Edward Thomas
Three Plays

Seren Drama

Edward Thomas Three Plays

House Of America
Flowers Of The Dead Red Sea
East From The Gantry

Edited by Brian Mitchell

seren

seren
is the book imprint of
Poetry Wales Press Ltd
Wyndham Street, Bridgend, Wales

First published in 1994
Reprinted 1998

ISBN 1-85411-113-2

A CIP record for this title is available from
the British Library

*The publisher works with the financial assistance of the
Arts Council of Wales*

Cover : Andy Dark

Printed in Palatino by CPD Wales

Contents

Iddyn Nhw
Wrtho Fe

Introduction

"Wales was invented by the Welsh because they desired its invention" claimed Edward Thomas in a conference speech later reproduced in *The Guardian* (September, 1991). If so, then as Professor Gwyn A. Williams insists in his book *When Was Wales*, the nation can be reinvented when the will exists. The playwright's purpose in this trilogy is no less than the creation of a new sense of Welshness, not through political action, but through art, specifically a contemporary, relevant, experimental, indigenous theatre. The plays in this volume are best received and most clearly understood as metaphors for Wales as it was, is and might be.

What is it that impedes this process of national reinvention? Lack of role models, certainly. "Where are our heroes? Our kings?" asks Sid Lewis in *House Of America*. "One answer, mate, we haven't got any". Vacant pedestals have been filled by media heroes, technologically delivered, mostly from the other side of the Atlantic. They intrude themselves into our most powerful and personal memories. In *East From The Gantry* a real-life glimpse of Telly Savalas demands to be recalled at the same time as the memory of a mother's death. Film images impose themselves on our local landscapes. Sid sees Merthyr through a filter of Mafia films and he and his brother jokingly identify *On The Waterfront* with the Mumbles. Such images may be held in affection, but they provide no nourishment. Magnus Magnusson will never arrive to tell Trampas's mother fantastic tales of old Iceland long into the night, and Tom Jones will never respond however many pairs of best French underwear Bella throws at him.

Sid Lewis in the first play in this trilogy has found in Jack Kerouac's *On The Road* a more sustaining story from a literary source; it is a story that will transform him initially, but eventually destroy him. Professor Barbara Hardy has written about every individual's need to create and tell his or her own stories. Making them is "...a primary act of the human mind... for we dream in narrative, day-dream in narrative, remember, anticipate, hope, despair, believe, doubt, plan, revise, criticise, construct, gossip, hate and love by narrative. In order to really live, we make up stories about ourselves and others, about the personal as well as the social past and future."* It is also, of course, one of the basic principles of psycho-analytic therapy that the right story can free the neurotic and give him control over himself. Indeed, we may all live more by fictions than by facts. Edward Thomas knows this very well, and the individual plays in his trilogy are linked by the attempts of his characters to find in their memories, or create in their imaginations, stories through which they can reinvent and assert themselves. Sid Lewis finds his story in the words and actions of the author of *On The Road*. Like Kerouac, the only models for him "...are the mad ones, mad to live, mad to talk, the ones who never yawn or say a commonplace thing, but burn, burn like fabulous yellow roman candles". What other sustaining belief can there be for a twenty-nine-year-old, who has only worked briefly during his life (as a grave-digger incidentally), living in a house of lies in a decaying industrial community? But Sid's obsession is not only with the ideas of the book; he believes he can relive the events of Kerouac's own life; in effect, become his personal god. Greek drama demanded above all a proper respect for the gods, and in this contemporary tragedy Sid's form of *hubris* can also lead only to disaster. As in the ill-fated house of Atreus, so in the house of America incest provokes murder, and Sid meets his death at the hands of the unbeliever Boyo, who sees no need for stories or for the process of acting. "Stories" as Mam says in the last performed version of the play, "they can make you, they can break you".

Flowers Of The Dead Red Sea has undergone a number of transformations. Since its original presentation, there have been restagings, a radio version, a chamber opera and ruthless editing by its author for publication. It emerges now as a leaner, cleaner metaphoric statement. The undergrowth of inessential characters and tangential philosophising have been cleared away and the central image of two men locked in a conflict of assertion and denial while the world falls about their heads is more clearly seen and strongly felt. What they are fighting to establish might be as trivial as the provenance of a bow-tie or as crucial as Mock's ignorance about his father and brother. The issues are not as central as the process itself. Mock and Joe must fight to reclaim truths or create fictions from their individual pasts; only then can they act and change. In this play naturalism is rejected with powerful effect; it is difficult to imagine a statement of such compelling resonance in the trappings of realistic stage presentation. By virtue of its lack of locality (there are no specific references to Wales or the Welsh in it), it works triumphantly not only as a lament for this nation ("a whole language, a way of life, a people drowning"), but also as a passionate rejection of a system of exploitation, a world sinking in its own blood and filth, and a cynicism that precludes action for change.

East From The Gantry is the most puzzling of Edward Thomas's plays. In a derelict house, a paranoid gun-toting husband cross-examines his wife about her supposed drunkenness and infidelities. She may or may not have burnt the house down. He is interrupted by a drifter who adopts the name and persona of a character from a sixties TV Western series. For good measure, all three share knowledge of a mysterious character (Martin Bratton) from an earlier Thomas play. The author himself has referred to the play's "fragile and dislocated nature" and describes it as "a play of possibilities where anything is possible". However, knowledge of the earlier two plays gives us guidelines for interpretation. Once again, the building blocks of the narrative are stories, in this instance, real memories of seminal events in the characters' lives. The play's most significant metaphor in performance is the physical act of uncovering concealed objects on the stage. Gradually, Ronnie and Bella dig down through layers of media saturation to the individual and shared memories which they must recover if they are to sustain their love in a rootless, estranging society. Finally, they achieve, if not fulfilment, at least an accommodation which is strong enough to enable

INTRODUCTION

them to look outward. Now, they can welcome into their relationship the drifter Trampas, who is lost somewhere between a valley home "which no longer continues to be" and the alienating city. Trampas/Billy can now reveal his true name and begin to gain a surer sense of his own identity. At the heart of this final play in the New Wales Trilogy, there is once again the insistence that reclaiming the past is necessary both for individuals and for nations.

Brian Mitchell
Editor

Barbara Hardy, 'Towards a Poetics of Fiction' from Novel: A Forum on Fiction, *published by Brown University, USA.*

House Of America

Notes to the Original Production

House of America was first performed as part of the radical writing season at St. Stephen's Theatre, Cardiff in May, 1988. The revised version toured South Wales, London and the Edinburgh Festival in 1989.

Cast

Mam	Sharon Morgan
Gwenny	Catherine Tregenna
Boyo	Richard Lynch
Sid	Russell Gomer
Labourer	Wyndham Price

Music by	Wyndham Price
Set and Lighting by	Ian Hill
Directed by	Edward Thomas

Act One

MOTHER: Thing is with a story is that you've got to be sure of the facts, or people will only get the wrong end of the stick, and you end up upsetting people without meaning to. I didn't mean any harm you say, but it's too late, the damage has been done. Then with some stories there's so much going on you don't know where to start, like if I tell to you what happened the night Clem, my husband left me. He went to America, that's the simple way of saying it, but there's more to it than that. Clem's a lorry driver see, well I don't know if he is now, haven't seen him in years, or heard from him. I remember him telling me one day the steering on the lorry went on the way to North Wales. "It's all the bends it is see," he said, "bend after bend, what I want is a straight road, America's got straight roads see, you get on and you never have to get off." It was the steering in his head that was gone, not the lorry. He said, "I want a new life in a house by the sea in California." I said, "You don't have to go to California to find a house by the sea, there's places here, in Wales." And he said, "Yeah, I know, but there'd be no room to park the lorry." Funny the things you remember on the day your husband leaves you. It had been one of those days, I'd been using the washing machine, but we had this cat see, called Brando, that was Clem's idea, Clem thought the world of Marlon Brando, but

13

what I thought was funny was that Marlon Brando had never heard of Clem. Anyway, when my back was turned, the cat decided to have a nap in the washing machine, and I didn't know it was in there, so I shut the door and started the machine, you can guess what happened, the cat couldn't swim. All of a sudden Clem came in, he loved the cat so I didn't know what to tell him, and I was just about to say something when he said, "I'm off" or something like that, and I said, "What do you mean, off?" "I'm going to America," he said, "tonight." And I said, "Oh." He was looking at me dumb, and said, "Well? What have you got to say?" "Brando's dead," I said, "I've just washed him to death. He got into the washing machine when I wasn't looking, it was an accident." "You did it on purpose," he said. "I'm definitely going." "I put him over there in the Tesco bag," I said. "He's still wet." Clem just looked at me and turned to go, and I said, "What about the kids?" "Keep them away from the washing machine." And he shut the door behind him. I haven't seen him since. So it was just me and the kids left, I told them where he'd gone and left it like that. Then I buried the cat down the bottom of the garden with a lollipop stick as a cross, buried him next to budgie Billy. You have to make do, see.

[Loud crashing, blasting noise. Stops.]

They're starting an Open Cast mine, it's enough to frighten any bugger.

[Music of Dionne Warwick singing 'Do You Know The Way To San Jose' as Mother exits. Boyo and Gwenny race in and build a house of cards.]

GWENNY: You ever heard of someone called Joyce Johnson, Boyo?

BOYO: No, should I?

GWENNY: Not really, no.

BOYO: What she about then?

GWENNY: No, I was just wondering.

BOYO: How's the cards coming on, then?

GWENNY: Not good, there's too much of a draught, see, look they're shaking.

BOYO: I don't know where it's coming from.

GWENNY: Nor me, but it's upsetting my cards.

BOYO: I know, the house is facing north, bound to get a draught.

GWENNY: That's got nothing to do with it, all I know is that now and then a draught blows, and rocks all the cards at the bottom of the pack, here, look, so they're all shaky, so the next card you put on is bound to bring the lot down, so you can't build on it, watch now.

[Gwenny carefully puts a card on. It wobbles a bit and they fall down. Boyo laughs.]

GWENNY: See what I mean.

BOYO: It's not the wind, mun, it's the table, it's wonky.

GWENNY: I'm telling you it's a draught, I can feel it.

[Boyo watches as she starts again.]

GWENNY: It's not going to beat me though.

[Boyo walks around half-heartedly looking for a draught. He picks up a book.]

BOYO: This your book?

GWENNY: Yeah, well no...

BOYO: Uh?

GWENNY: It's Sid's, but he lent it to me.

BOYO: Jesus, he hasn't read a book in years, has he?

GWENNY: Don't know, but he likes that one.

BOYO: What's this bloke called... Jack...

GWENNY: Kerouac.

BOYO: Never heard of him.

GWENNY: He's from America.

BOYO: "...The Beat Generation's classic novel of sex, jazz and freedom...." Sounds alright to me, I knew Sid liked two of them, one he doesn't get very often and the other one he thinks he's got, but I didn't know he liked jazz.

GWENNY: He does, and I do, but he hasn't got the money to buy the records.

BOYO: News to me.

GWENNY: He went to the Brecon Jazz Festival last year remember?

BOYO: Oh yeah, but I thought he went because of the booze, and a lift on a motorbike.

GWENNY: No, he likes the music too. Charlie Parker he likes. You can borrow the book after me, Boyo.

BOYO: Yeah, I'll have to. *[throws down the book]*

GWENNY: He'll be back before long now... hope he gets those jobs for you.

BOYO: What jobs?

GWENNY: The ones on the new Open Cast, hasn't he told you?

BOYO: No, I heard about something though, but no, Sid didn't tell me.

GWENNY: They want labourers, local labourers, Sid's gone to see some Irish bloke about it.

BOYO: Limerick, you mean.

GWENNY: That's him, he reckons he's all right.

BOYO: Jesus, why didn't he tell me then?

GWENNY: I thought he did.

BOYO: Been telling you all his secrets has he?

          [Gwenny looks away.]

GWENNY: He told me he thought he was getting old before his time.

BOYO: That's my fault that is, I told him his hair was falling out and his teeth needed filling.

GWENNY: No, I think he meant it.

          [The card house collapses again.]

GWENNY: Oh, Christ, look it's happened again.

          [Boyo laughs.]

GWENNY: That's it. I've had enough.

BOYO: Hey, I don't want any jibs.

GWENNY: I'm not jibbing, but it's turning into a life's work.

          [Gwenny takes a chair and stands on it looking out the window. Boyo takes over with the cards.]

GWENNY: What would happen if all the planets round the sun slow down then, Boyo?

BOYO: Hey, mun, what sort of question is that?

GWENNY: C'mon, give me an answer.

BOYO: I don't know.

GWENNY: Heard it on the radio I did, the earth is travelling at eighteen miles a second round the sun.

BOYO: How many potatoes were made into chips last year — keeps you awake at nights doesn't it?

GWENNY: Don't laugh, it's true.

BOYO: They give you tablets for stuff like that, you know that?

GWENNY: But, if all the planets... like earth right, decide to slow down, well, we'd just fall into the sun and burn.

BOYO: I'd better keep my fingers crossed then or pray to Jesus or something.

MOTHER: Jesus is a busy man.

BOYO: Uh?

[*Mother appears at the back of the stage.*]

MOTHER: I said Jesus is a busy man, you can't always get through to him when you call, but he knows me. I say Jesus, it's Mrs Lewis from Wales, and if I'm lucky, on a good night he'll answer. Was it you who wanted him, Boyo?

BOYO: No, me and Gwenny was just talking.

MOTHER: Like I got through to him the other night, asking forgiveness, but I wasn't at my best, but you know what he said, he said there was so much going on down there it's hard to keep track, and if it carried on like this he'd have to go and put his head in the sand, Jesus himself.

BOYO: Well, if he feels like that what have we got to worry about, innit, uh, Gwen?

GWENNY: Oh, yeah... yeah....

MOTHER: I mean with all those things on his mind he could hit the bottle, couldn't he?

GWENNY: They've probably got beer in heaven see, mam.

MOTHER: All I'm saying is that he'll have to watch out, we can't have him drunk in charge of the world, can we?

18

BOYO: What you want him to forgive you for then?

MOTHER: That's between him, me, and the deep blue sea. Doing tricks, Boyo?

[She knocks the cards over.]

BOYO: Oi, mun, what you want to do that for? I was getting somewhere then.

GWENNY: There's too much of a draught. Anyway, mam, it's my trick.

BOYO: No need to tip them over though.

MOTHER: I want to talk anyway.

GWENNY: What about?

MOTHER: My room's been painted blue.

BOYO: So?

MOTHER: It's the wrong colour.

GWENNY: It's been blue for as long as I can remember, mam.

MOTHER: Nobody's painted it behind my back then.

BOYO: No, what do you think?

MOTHER: Don't make fun. I wouldn't have asked it I didn't think it. I'm not funny yet.

GWENNY: You probably painted it yourself, mam.

MOTHER: It's the wrong colour I say, shows up the dirt too much. Red's my colour.

BOYO: What you mean, mam, there's no dirt there, you've been washing it every day for the last month.

MOTHER: It won't come off I tell you, if it had been painted red nobody'd see it, wouldn't see anything. Blue's the wrong colour. It's the Open Cast, it was all right before the Open Cast came, it's the worst thing that could have happened here, and I'm getting careless, been all right for years. If anybody goes to the shops buy some red paint for my room, got to be red. Damn Open Cast.

[Boyo and Gwenny exchange glances.]

BOYO: It's here now, so that's that.

GWENNY: And the boys need jobs.

MOTHER: Wet behind the ears, the two of you.

BOYO: Hey listen, I'm not going to argue. Oh, the bastard thing's fallen again.

GWENNY: I don't know what you're bothering for tonight, Boyo, you'll never do it.

MOTHER: It'll change everything.

[Fade in Sam and Dave's 'Soul Man' as Sid enters exuberantly.]

MOTHER: Turn the music down, I'm trying to talk.

[No response. Eventually she goes to the record player herself and turns the music off.]

SID: Hey, mun, I was getting into that.

MOTHER: How old are you?

SID: What sort of question is that, mother?

MOTHER: You're nearly thirty, and I'm trying to talk.

SID: Hey come on, not now, not now, I've got news.

MOTHER: What news?

SID: News... News... News....

GWENNY: What, Sid, what?

SID: Boyo, me and you are going to Hirwaun in that three legged car of yours to sign up for jobs as labourers, and the money, brother, is sweet.

MOTHER: Not on the Open Cast.

BOYO: Hey, Sid, that's great.

GWENNY: Great.

BOYO: You saw Limerick?

SID: Yep, and he reckons we've got a good chance too.

BOYO: What time have we got to be there?

SID: First thing in the morning.

GWENNY: What time's that?

SID: I don't know, nine o'clock I suppose.

BOYO: I'll have to put the alarm on.

SID: Five years' work, then they fill the hole in, plant some grass and trees and you can't tell anybody's been there, and then fly across the sea.

GWENNY: We can go to America on that.

SID: Too right we can, c'mon, who fancies a pint, celebrate it? Gwenny, you coming?

BOYO: We'll have a job each now.

MOTHER: Women were his weakness, he didn't smoke, didn't drink much and he couldn't help the way he looked. Everybody thought he was handsome, didn't have much of a temper, just had a soft spot for women, that was his trouble.

SID: What she talking about now, for Christ sake?

GWENNY: What's wrong, mam?

BOYO: What you talking about, mam?

MOTHER: Your father, who do you think I'm talking about?

BOYO: What's he got to do with anything now?

SID: C'mon, let's go, she's only having a rant.

MOTHER: Looked like a film star he did, like Errol Flynn, I was lucky, I've told Mr Snow all about him.

GWENNY: Mr Snow?

SID: Who's he?

MOTHER: Haven't I told you about Mr Snow?

BOYO: No, you....

MOTHER She was a floozy... your father ran away with a floozy. I was too busy looking after you three, he always said I had no time for him, and then the floozy got her hands on him behind my back. He was a dreamer and he fell for the glitter.

GWENNY: It's all right, mam.

MOTHER: No, it's not all right, the Open Cast will dig up everything in sight, and I'll be lost. Let sleeping dogs lie, it's been a long time, history is history.

BOYO: What you trying to say, mam?

MOTHER: All gone.

SID: Something to do with the old man.

MOTHER: But I've already told you, haven't I? He's in America, you know he's in America, don't you?

GWENNY: Yes.

BOYO: Where else is he then, mam?

MOTHER: Nowhere... that's where he went to, left us in the lurch, wasn't my fault, could have happened to anyone, but mind you this is where he belongs... but he couldn't see, this was his home but he didn't know, and he'll come back here one day.

GWENNY: You think so?

MOTHER: Definite, he won't be in America forever, liked John Wayne too much he did, so he went to the Wild West with his floozy.

SID: Frontier man the old man see, Boyo, took his horse and his woman, headed West and built a ranch for himself.

[Sid laughs.]

BOYO: Shut up mun, Sid, don't wind her up.

MOTHER: She had relations out there... you talking behind my back?

SID: No, no, just saying to Boyo, that's right I said.

GWENNY: C'mon, mam, come and have a lie down, you'll feel better then.

MOTHER: You're not going to work on the Open Cast, are you?

SID: Yeah... interview's tomorrow.

MOTHER: You can't, hear me, you can't, it'll be the end of us.

SID: It's a job. A job is a job.

MOTHER: Listen to you, still boys.

SID: Hey, I'm pushing thirty.

BOYO: He's only pulling your leg, mam, all the jobs have gone. Here, let Gwenny take you for a lie down.

MOTHER: I don't trust you boys, you're not listening to me.

GWENNY: C'mon, mam.

[Gwenny leads Mother away.]

MOTHER: I'm warning you.

[Mother and Gwenny exit.]

SID: She's going off her rocker, mate, she's getting worse, and she's too young to be senile.

BOYO: I didn't know she was this bad, I thought it was her nerves.

SID: No way. I'm telling you she's losing her marbles. The men in the white coats will be knocking on the door and taking her away if she's not careful.

BOYO: She's not that bad yet, we'll have to keep an eye on

her, that's all.

SID: What she bring the old man up for now?

BOYO: I don't know, she hasn't mentioned him for years, — not like that anyway.

SID: Maybe she's heard from him.

BOYO: How?

SID: I don't know, written her a letter or something.

BOYO: Why should he bother now when we haven't heard a peep from him since he went?

SID: You never know.

BOYO: I haven't seen any letters.

SID: Hey, he might be writing to ask us to go out there on a visit.

BOYO: Bollocks to him, I wouldn't go.

SID: You're off your head, big country, mun, get a job there and settle down.

BOYO: We don't even know where he lives, mun.

SID: Fuck, a trip to America, be all right I reckon.

BOYO: Might be for you, but I don't see it that way.

SID: Don't be so miserable, mun, it's only an idea.

BOYO: Where's he been for the last ten years, that's what I want to know. If he thought anything of us he'd have written earlier, as it stands now he can drop dead. I don't ever want to see the bastard, fuck him and fuck America.

SID: Don't get so heavy, mun, things change, got to change with the times, Boyo, got to give him a chance, he's our old man, mun.

BOYO: What chance did he give us, Sid, uh?

SID: That was a long time ago, we've all grown up now,

and he probably had his reasons.

[Lights fade on Boyo and Sid. Lights up on Mother and Gwenny on another part of stage.]

MOTHER: Do you know who you are?

GWENNY: Yes, mam, Gwenny.

MOTHER: Do you know who I am?

GWENNY: You're my mother.

MOTHER: And what's a mother, Gwenny?

GWENNY: You are.

MOTHER: Are you sure? Have I done a good job, have I brought you up all right?

GWENNY: Yes, course you have.

MOTHER: Things aren't right, is it me?

GWENNY: No.

MOTHER: And those are your brothers?

GWENNY: Yes, mam, what's wrong, tell me.

MOTHER: Everything, and I can't.

GWENNY: You can trust me, mam.

MOTHER: Do you know what home is?

GWENNY: Yes.

MOTHER: What is it?

GWENNY: It's where we live, mam, all of us.

MOTHER: Where is it?

GWENNY: Here, where do you think it is?

MOTHER: I've done my best, and I'm not that old, you now I've done my best, don't you? Everything I a.. vas to help you three.

GWENNY: What are you saying?

25

MOTHER: Nothing, no more, leave me alone now, I'm all right.

GWENNY: Mam... I can...

MOTHER: Leave me alone, I need time to think.

[Mother exits. Gwenny rejoins Sid and Boyo.]

BOYO: What did she want, Gwen?

GWENNY: I don't know, she's upset about something, but she won't say.

SID: She all right now?

GWENNY: She's gone to her room.

BOYO: She doesn't want the Open Cast, that's what started it.

GWENNY: Her nerves are really bad.

BOYO: Playing tricks with her mind.

SID: Listen to doctor Quack here.

BOYO: Could happen.

GWENNY: I thought she'd be glad to see you getting some work.

SID: Rambling she is, she'll be all right in a bit — and I've had enough of this crypticness, who's coming down the pub?

BOYO: Bit awkward now, innit? One of us will have to stay and look after her.

GWENNY: Don't look at me, it's always me.

SID: And I'm dying of thirst.

BOYO: We can't leave her on her own, mun.

GWENNY: He's right, Sid, we'll all have to stay.

SID: That's typical, that's fucking typical.

BOYO: She can't help being ill, mun.

SID: Putting it on she is, I'm telling you, any excuse to keep us in the house. We're not youngsters for Christ sake.

GWENNY: We can't leave her whether she's joking or not.

SID: She always comes up with something to put the mockers on things, a Spaniard in the works.

BOYO: Don't be a bastard, Sid, will you?

SID: Celebration this is supposed to be, when was the last time you heard of jobs coming up?

BOYO: It's not the point, is it?

SID: I'm just saying, aren't I?

GWENNY: C'mon, there's no point arguing about it, why don't we go down the off licence and get some cans instead, then we'll have a little party, and we can look after her.

SID: Give that woman an O level. Gwenny, I love you. Put some pennies on the table.

[Boyo laughs.]

BOYO: You're a bastard, aren't you?

SID: C'mon, Boyo, put your cash on the table.

GWENNY: Who's going down then?

SID: I'll go, and someone else to give me a hand.

GWENNY: I'll go, I wouldn't mind a walk.

BOYO: Hey, buy some Jaffa Cakes too. I wouldn't mind some Jaffa Cakes.

SID: See what we can do, brother.

[Sid and Gwenny exit. Boyo lights a cigarette and goes to stand at the window. Mother appears in the shadows and watches him.]

MOTHER: See anything special out there, Boyo?

BOYO: Oh, I didn't hear you... yeah... have a look.

MOTHER: What's out there?

BOYO: There's a sheep out there look, limping.

MOTHER: Where?

BOYO: Down there look, by the fence, — it's hopping around.

MOTHER: It's lost, that's what it is.

BOYO: Can't keep up with the flock when you've got three legs, can you? The farmer'll send it to the slaughter house, won't he?

MOTHER: Not if it's going to lamb, he'll wait for her to lamb and then get rid of her.

BOYO: Hard life being a sheep, innit? *[laughs]*

          [Pause.]

MOTHER: Where's your brother and sister?

BOYO: Gone to get some booze.

          [Mother studies him.]

MOTHER: Do you love me, Boyo?

BOYO: Uh?

MOTHER: You heard.

BOYO: What you asking me that for?

MOTHER: I want to know.

BOYO: Yeah....

MOTHER: I want to hear you say it.

BOYO: Oh come on, mun, give me a break.

MOTHER: I want to hear you say it.

BOYO: I love you, all right. You're my mother, aren't you?

MOTHER: You're not going to forget about me, are you?

BOYO: No, what do you think?

MOTHER: I wouldn't have asked you if I knew.

BOYO: Well you know now, right?

MOTHER: So you're not going to send me away.

BOYO: What do we want to do that for?

MOTHER: Because my mind's not right, my nerves are bad, you know they are, I'm not myself.

BOYO: I know that, but you'll get better, this is your home, mun, this is where you belong.

MOTHER: Would you still love me if you knew I'd done something wrong, something bad?

BOYO: Yeah, course I would.

MOTHER: No matter what it was?

BOYO: I'd know you had your reasons.

MOTHER: Good boy.

BOYO: Why did you ask?

MOTHER: I wanted to be sure.

            [Pause.]

MOTHER: Listen, you've got to promise me something.

BOYO: What?

MOTHER: You and your brother. I don't want you to work on that Open Cast.

BOYO: Oh, come on now, why not?

MOTHER: I'm telling you.

BOYO: It's work, mam, it won't come that near the house, they're only digging the mountains, they don't want the house as well. Is that what you're afraid of?

MOTHER: This house is all we've got, you just said, I heard

29

you.

BOYO: Coal they want, not houses.

MOTHER: When they start digging they'll find it.

BOYO: Find what?

MOTHER: Your history, part of your history is on that mountain.

BOYO: I don't follow you.

MOTHER: It's lying there, quiet, not making any noise, they'll start digging, and that will be that — all hell will break loose. Huh, this house is full of lies, but I suppose it's kept us together.

BOYO: What lies?

MOTHER: It's kept us together and that's the main thing, you told me yourself, and now they're going to dig the mountains and the mountains are full of lies and this house will start rocking, and I'm telling you, Boyo, you'll have to be strong, you'll have to remember who you are and where you are, and as long as you've got that you'll be all right but you've got to stick together, you listening?

BOYO: What you telling me for?

MOTHER: Because I've been watching you, and Gwenny and Sid. I know they want to go to America after him, but there's nothing there, and Gwenny's been writing him letters.

BOYO: How do you know?

MOTHER: I've got eyes, I can see, you're on my side, I heard you call your father a bastard, you said it tonight. Do you think I haven't got ears?

BOYO: Yeah, on the side of your head by the looks of it.

MOTHER: *[grabs him]* Don't laugh at your mother.

BOYO: I'm not laughing, leave me go.

[Mother leaves him go.]

BOYO: What's my father got to do with it?

MOTHER: Everything. He's not in America, he's never been to America, all he ever did was dream about America.

BOYO: Everybody knows he went to America.

MOTHER: Lies, all lies. It was the only way to keep us together.

BOYO: Then where the hell is he?

[Silence.]

BOYO: Mam? Answer me?

MOTHER: I was only joking. You'll have to be strong, and you said you'll always love me and I believe you.

BOYO: Where is he, mam?

[Mother kisses him.]

MOTHER: Don't tell your brother and sister, not yet, but the time will come, you'll have to be strong.

BOYO: Tell me where he is.

MOTHER: You told me you didn't know who Mr Snow was, well I'll tell you. Some people call him interference, you know? On the telly. But I call him Mr Snow.

[Mother walks off.]

BOYO: Oh Jesus....

[Lights change. Boyo, Sid and Gwenny are drinking, in a party state. The Doors 'Love Her Madly' plays in the background.]

BOYO: I'm telling you, Sid, John Cale never played with the Doors, he was with Velvet Underground, ask Gwenny.

GWENNY: Boyo's right, Sid, Velvet Underground.

SID: Oh balls to it anyway, Lou Reed's better than John Cale. I said, hey babe, take a walk on the wild side.

GWENNY: I'm dancing on my own, who's going to dance?

BOYO: I can't dance, or I'll hic... fall over.

        [Laughter.]

BOYO: Hey, the other thing about John Cale was, he's Welsh.

SID: No, he's not, he's American, New York band.

BOYO: I'm telling you he comes from Ponty or somewhere.

SID: Bullshit, Boyo, talking crap.

BOYO: You ask Cat next time you see him.

SID: What does he know?

BOYO: He's fucking tuned the piano for Lindisfarne, that's what he knows, last time they were in the Rank in Town.

SID: Aye, but look what happened to them after that, they haven't had a hit since.

BOYO: Not the point, Sid.

SID: Cat, what does he know, the only deaf piano tuner in the country, and I don't care if Cale came from fucking Ystrad, he's living in New York now, and I bet you that's where he'll stay, huh, can you imagine Lou Reed walking 'round Ystrad — all right Lou, how's it going, wus, on the Wild Side — not cool enough for him, no way, probably never even heard of Wales.

BOYO: He don't know nothing that's why.

GWENNY: C'mon, come and dance.

        [Boyo gets up and falls over. General laughter.]

BOYO: Jesus, my legs have had it, what's that rocket fuel

you bought?

[Sid gets up and struggles to dance with Gwenny. Boyo mimes a Gerry Anderson puppet, drawing a very wobbly imaginary gun.]

BOYO: Butteeeeeeeeeaaaaaaawwwwwwww.

SID: Quick, Gwenny, duck, the Mysterons are here.

BOYO: *[singing]* Captain Scarlet, indestructible.

           [Sid wobbly shoots back at Boyo.]

BOYO: Ahh... he got me... *[falls over]* Oi, Sid... Thunderbird one, wus, in trouble.

SID: What you think then, Lady Penelope?

GWENNY: Drive me to the sun, Parker.

SID: Yes, milady.

           [Sid picks Gwenny up and runs around the room, the music fades and Mother is standing in the shadows.]

GWENNY: Oh look, it's mam. Put me down, Parker.

SID: Yes, milady.

GWENNY: Feeling better?

SID: We're having a party here, are you staying or going, mam?

MOTHER: What time is it?

BOYO: Not late, mam, you better?

SID: She's going to stay and have a drink.

MOTHER: Been playing, you three?

GWENNY: Come and sit down here, look, by me.

MOTHER: I came to see about the fire.

SID: Don't worry about the fire, plenty of fire here, hot.

MOTHER: Can't let it go out, needs wood, we'll have to keep it in. I'll go and get some wood.

BOYO: Not now, mam, can't go out now, and there's plenty of... hic... wood.

SID: See, the fire's happy.

GWENNY: Come and sit here, mam.

SID: Yeah, we're celebrating. Job interviews tomorrow, mun, have a drink.

[Gwenny pours Mother a drink.]

MOTHER: Is there a film on or what?

SID: A film?

GWENNY: We've been dancing, but you want to see a film.

BOYO: Yeah, go on, Sid, go and put a film on.

SID: Aye, I'm knackered anyway.

GWENNY: Good job we've got a video.

MOTHER: I didn't know we had one, where did it come from?

BOYO: Ask no questions and I'll tell you no lies.

SID: Same place as the ironing board, the camera, Gwenny's jacket....

GWENNY: We don't need a list, Sid.

SID: That's where they all came from.

GWENNY: What sort of film do you want, mam?

MOTHER: Have you got any musicals?

BOYO: No, mam, no musicals.

SID: It's all right, problem solved... found one.

BOYO: What you got?

SID: You'll see now.

GWENNY: I know, 'The Godfather'.

SID: How did you guess?

MOTHER: Who's the Godfather?

SID: Marlon Brando, mam.

MOTHER: Oh... your father liked Marlon Brando.

BOYO: Film about the mafia.

MOTHER: The mafia?

SID: Yeah, you know, ice-cream sellers in Merthyr.

            [Laughter.]

MOTHER: What are you laughing at?

GWENNY: Nothing, mam, nothing.

SID: It's a good film, here it comes now, look.

GWENNY: You'll have to rewind it, Sid, it's in the middle.

MOTHER: Those boys don't come from Merthyr.

SID: I was joking.

GWENNY: They're Italian gangsters... hic... in America.

MOTHER: What they doing in America then?

BOYO: Don't wind her up, Sid.

GWENNY: There he is look.

MOTHER: Oh, Marlon Brando, he's put a lot of weight on.

BOYO: He can't act, mun, he's a mumbler.

MOTHER: We used to watch him when he was younger.

SID: He's no mumbler, Boyo, he's got style.

BOYO: What did he say then?

GWENNY: Something about Palermo.

MOTHER: Where's Palermo?

BOYO: Mumble, mumble, mumble.

SID: Can you remember some of his films, mam?

MOTHER: No, but we watched them, let's see now.

GWENNY: 'The Wild Ones'.

SID: That's not a Brando film.

MOTHER: Ugh, what have they put that horse's head in that man's bed for?

SID: It was his racehorse.

[Boyo gets himself more drink.]

GWENNY: You've got to know the story, Sid should rewind it back to the start.

SID: All right, hang on I'll rewind it.

MOTHER: Wasn't the film called 'On The River' or something?

SID: 'On The Waterfront' that's what it was, great film.

BOYO: 'On The Mumbles' it should have been.

GWENNY: Don't listen to him, he's being funny.

MOTHER: All the people in this film are going backwards.

BOYO: No wonder, they've got Marlon Brando in it.

SID: There, look, back to the start.

BOYO: 'Cos you can't have 'On The Waterfront' without the Mumbles can you.

[Boyo laughs out loud, and nearly falls over.]

GWENNY: What's wrong with you, Boyo, be quiet and watch the film.

SID: Can't hold his booze that's what it is.

MOTHER: They've shot somebody now.

BOYO: Who wants to be a film star anyway?

GWENNY: Jealous he is.

BOYO: Pretending to be somebody else for a living, lies, all lies.

SID: Shut up, mun, and watch the film.

BOYO: It's a Mickey Mouse film.

SID: Any beer left in that, Gwenny?

MOTHER: Lot of killing going on, a musical I wanted.

[Boyo starts to do a Brando impersonation.]

MOTHER: What's Boyo doing?

GWENNY: Bad impressions of film stars.

SID: That one's called trying to be sober when you're pissed.

BOYO: What did I say then?

SID: Wasn't listening.

BOYO: You didn't understand me see, did you?

GWENNY: You weren't doing it properly.

BOYO: Proves my point, he's a mumbler.

MOTHER: What did you say, Boyo?

BOYO: I said "I could have been a contender, I could have been somebody."

MOTHER: What did he say?

SID: He said it wrong, watch the film and he'll stop.

MOTHER: Not my kind of film.

SID: Oh Jesus.

GWENNY: Shsss Sid.

BOYO: *[shouting]* I said I could have been somebody, hear me. I could have been a boxer, or a farmer, or a miner, or I don't know, something real, something to get your teeth into, not lies, lies, actors, films fucking cloud cuckoo buckoo...

[He stumbles and falls. Sid turns the film off.]

GWENNY: I was watching that.

SID: Forget it.

MOTHER: Not my cup of tea.

SID: There's something wrong with Boyo's head.

[Sid walks over to Boyo who's prostrate on the floor.]

SID: What you do that for, you bastard?

MOTHER: Stop swearing, the two of you.

[Sid kicks Boyo when he's on the floor. Boyo retaliates and kicks back.]

GWENNY: C'mon, the two of you, stop it. Like kids you are.

BOYO: He kicked me.

[Sid walks away and swigs a bottle.]

MOTHER: I don't want any fighting in this house, got to stick together.

SID: Can't hold his beer that's all, alky he is.

BOYO: Who do you think you are then? Rambo? One hundred and eighty pints a night.

GWENNY: Stop it, the two of you, like kids.

MOTHER: Time for everybody to go to bed.

BOYO: Yeah... bed.

SID: You know what your problem is, Boyo, you don't know how to swing, you're stuck in a groove, mate.

BOYO: At least I'm not losing my hair and going old before my time.

[Sid throws a can at Boyo.]

BOYO: Missed.

SID: Let's just wait and see who gets a job tomorrow, that's all I've got to say. That's depending on whether that car of yours can start.

BOYO: It'll start like a bird.

SID: Bet you we'll have to get a bus.

BOYO: I'm not getting involved in this crap.

MOTHER: Bed, boys and girl.

BOYO: Don't worry, I'm going.

SID: Goodnight, brother.

BOYO: Goodnight.

          [Boyo laughs and exits.]

MOTHER: You two shouldn't argue.

SID: What did he want to buy a car with three wheels for, it's only three quarters of a car, typical of him, he's not all there.

GWENNY: C'mon, Sid, give me a hand clearing up.

SID: How are you so sober then, Gwen?

GWENNY: Don't drink as much as you. You two shouldn't wind each other up.

SID: Him it is.

MOTHER: You should stick together.

SID: I mean fancy going 'On The Road' in Boyo's car — wouldn't get you as far as Swansea.

MOTHER: What you going on the road for, where you going?

GWENNY: If they get these jobs tomorrow, mam, we'll all be able to go on the road — holiday somewhere.

MOTHER: I'd like that.

SID: Yeah, fly to America, hire a car, and drive right across it, chasing the sun.

MOTHER: America?

[Gwenny makes eyes at Sid.]

SID: I've been reading this book, see, mam, about these two blokes who drive across America, hitching, and mad they are, looking for a dream... Jack Kerouac his name is.

MOTHER: Oh...?

GWENNY: C'mon, Sid, help me clear up.

SID: We could do that, mam, call in on dad.

[Pause.]

SID: What you think? You've got his address and stuff.

[Gwenny tips a bottle deliberately on the floor.]

GWENNY: Oh... shit... you'll have to give me a hand, Sid.

MOTHER: I can't go, wouldn't be welcome, his floozy'll be there with him.

[Gwenny forces Sid to help her. They clear up.]

MOTHER: The Open Cast is going to change everything. *[she gets up]* Goodnight all.

GWENNY: Goodnight, mam.

SID: Goodnight.

[She exits. There are sounds of industry and heavy machinery. Lights fade.]

Act Two

[Sid and Boyo enter. They are on a mountainside.]

SID: That's it, Boyo, that is fucking it, that's the straw that bastard breaks the beaver's back.

BOYO: Camel, Sid, camel.

SID: Don't give me pernickety, I'm telling you straight, mun, camel — you hear me — camel.

BOYO: Don't let it get you down, wus.

SID: Get me down? I'm telling you I've played it by the book and it gets you nowhere, it's fucking typical.

BOYO: Could have got up earlier I suppose.

SID: Is that all you've got to say? Don't kid yourself, Boyo, we could have queued up since last week, and I bet you they'd have found eight labourers to do the job before us. All over the country there's always eight labourers or eight shop assistants who get the job before you. They used to say I was too young, now we're too bastard old. That was the last chance I'm giving them to give me, Sid Lewis, a job. They've wrecked my plans and I've got to do something about it.

BOYO: They were Mickey Mouse jobs anyway, a dog could have done them.

SID: Anything with no brain and a coat could have done them, that's the problem, Boyo, everything round here is Mickey Mouse, wus. Division four, small time, second class toys.

41

BOYO: The only way to look at it is to forget about it.

SID: I mean look at this, listen to this, "No man shall operate any digging machinery of any kind without a labourer being present at all times." In other words, you stand there like a lemon watching the machine. Bollocks — it's all bollocks.

BOYO: Sid, mun, I....

SID: I mean who wants to be a labourer for those shits? The least you can do is drive one of those machines. Imagine, there you are right, labouring in the middle of winter, tipping down with rain right, and you're in this black basin, haven't talked to a soul all day; so you look at the bloke in the machine and he's all snug and warm in his cab, and he calls you over, so you go over thinking he might want a chat and the crack. So you knock on his window and you ask him what he wants, and he turns round and says fuck off, I don't want to talk to you.

[Boyo laughs.]

BOYO: Remember when we were grave digging? The squally showers.

SID: Oh they were bastards. I tell you that's what's causing all the depression, that's what's affecting mam's nerves, I tell you.

BOYO: You never know where you stand, that's the worst with squally showers, like you never knew whether it was worth putting a coat on or not, like you're shovelling away, digging some poor bastard's grave in the rain and all of a sudden it stops, and you've got your coat on and you get too hot, so you take it off, then next thing you know it starts to rain again, so you put it back on again, and after a couple of days doing that you don't know if you've got your bastard coat on or off, so you're either boiling or wet, either way you can't make up your mind anyway, so you're a prime candidate for a cold, so you're off work, ending up hot, cold... confused.

SID: Depressed.

BOYO: Depressed... yeah....

SID: Poor.

BOYO: Yeah... Coughing your lungs up, and you don't know who you are or whether you're coming or going, and you don't even know after all that who the hell's hole it is you're digging to bury him.

SID: Good job we're shot of that job, Boyo.

BOYO: And the labouring on the Cast, it's the only way to look at it, and I'll tell you another thing — mam wasn't keen on us working there in the first place.

SID: Why not?

[Pause.]

BOYO: Oh, you know how she is, worried about us.

SID: That money would have paid for a trip to America, Boyo.

BOYO: You wouldn't have gone anyway.

SID: How do you know?

BOYO: Because you're a fucking dreamer, that's why.

SID: No way, mate, I've been thinking about it, it's been in my head for ages, I'd be there, find out where the old man is, I'd be there. I was talking to Gwenny about it, she said she'd come too.

BOYO: Talked to her about it, have you?

SID: Yeah, and you know what?

BOYO: What?

SID: She's written the old man a few letters.

BOYO: How do you know?

SID: I was there when she wrote them.

BOYO: Where did she get the address then?

SID: She pestered mam for it.

BOYO: He hasn't answered though, has he?

SID: No, but the main thing is she's got the address.

          [Pause.]

SID: Plenty of work there too, Boyo, plenty of space, sun, sand, fancy riding across it chasing the sun on a Harley Davidson, money in your pocket, tiger in your tank, Hendrix on the Walkman — no helmet — just free and moving West.

BOYO: You can do that in Pembroke, Sid.

SID: Pembroke, don't give me Pembroke, what happens when you reach the sea, the end of the line?

BOYO: I don't know, you lie down on the beach and look at the sky.

SID: Watching the rain come down, no way, you wait for low tide you do and ride hell for leather across the Atlantic.

BOYO: Can I ask you one question, Sid?

SID: Yeah, anything, say.

BOYO: Have you got a bike?

SID: Don't give me that shit now, will you?

BOYO: Well you haven't got a bike have you, and you're not far off thirty and you're skint.

SID: I don't want to know all right? All I know is that I wasn't born to live in this... in rain... it's not natural, I tell you I could live in a tent if the sun was shining.

BOYO: And you'd wake up in the morning singing Cat Stevens' songs — 'Morning has broken...'.

SID: I tell you, I've been born in the wrong country, I have.

BOYO: You reckon, do you?

SID: Yeah, I reckon. If I had to answer a straight question, I'd have to say I wish I'd been born someone else, somewhere else.

BOYO: Oh yeah? ...like who?

SID: I don't know... someone else.

[Pause.]

Jack Kerouac.

BOYO: Never heard of him.

SID: He wrote this book I'm reading, *On the Road.*

BOYO: Are you telling me you want to write a book or what? You, who hasn't read a book since he left school.

SID: No, mun, not write a book.

BOYO: What then?

SID: Have a life where something happens, like he went all round America, him and his mate, crazy bastards they were.

BOYO: Yeah?

SID: Yeah, I tell you something he said now, he said "...the only ones for me are the mad ones, mad to live, mad to talk, the ones who never yawn or say a commonplace thing, but burn, burn, burn, like fabulous yellow roman candles..." What you think of that, then?

BOYO: Yeah, it's good. American, was he?

SID: All his life.

BOYO: You don't have to go to America to find crazy bastards though, do you?

SID: He was looking for a dream, Boyo, chasing a dream.

BOYO: Did he find it?

SID: I don't know, I haven't finished the book yet — you can read it after me.

BOYO: Yeah, tell me when you've finished it.

SID: That's what the old man did, I reckon.

BOYO: What?

SID: Chased his dreams.

BOYO: Women he was after, Sid, not dreams.

SID: He saw his chance and wooooofffff he took it, can't blame him, can you?

BOYO: He was a bastard, Sid, he had responsibilities.

SID: Only half the size of his dreams, mate, that's the way I see it, fuckin' land of opportunity, innit? Nobody thought Tom Jones was a bastard and he went there.

BOYO: He did it 'cos of the tax, and anyway he's back now in the Vale.

SID: I thought you liked him, Boyo, just up your street, "Green, green grass of home..." and that.

BOYO: Don't be so soft, will you.

SID: I've heard you playing his records, mate, him and Elvis.

BOYO: The Tom Jones is for mam, Sid, the Elvis ones are mine. Elvis is the king, always was and always will be.

SID: That's it, see Boyo, that's what I'm talking about, he was the king, but look at Wales, where's its kings, where's our heroes? ...one answer, mate, we haven't got any. I mean let's face it, Boyo, Harry Secombe isn't a bloke I'd stand in the rain for, is he?

[Boyo laughs.]

Is he?

BOYO: You know what, you haven't half got a gob on you, Sid.

SID: It's called facing facts, wus, telling the truth about the way things are.

BOYO: Harry Secombe never said he was a hero.

SID: No, and he's fucking right too. No, I tell you, mate, I've had it up to here, from now on I'm going to do things my way.

BOYO: Your way?

SID: My way. The Sid Lewis experience.

[Sid and Boyo exit as Frank Sinatra's 'My Way' plays. Lights up on mam looking out of a window. Gwenny is looking at photographs.]

MOTHER: Do you like Frank Sinatra, Gwenny?

GWENNY: Mmmm.

MOTHER: I'm glad you like him.

GWENNY: Why's that?

MOTHER: I'll be playing a lot of him from now on.

GWENNY: Will you?

MOTHER: Yes, to hide the noise.

GWENNY: What noise?

MOTHER: The noise from the Open Cast.

GWENNY: We can't only play Frank Sinatra, mam, I've got records too.

MOTHER: I'll get to know them off by heart then.

[*Pause.*]

I'm glad the boys didn't get the jobs.

GWENNY: I'm not, we could have done with the money.

MOTHER: Money's not everything.

GWENNY: Sid was upset, mam, and he already thinks he's getting old before his time.

MOTHER: He'll get over it, something will come.

GWENNY: He wanted to go to America, mam.

MOTHER: To see your father?

GWENNY: Yes, and I would have gone with him, but it's all gone wrong now.

MOTHER: What about Boyo?

GWENNY: He said he didn't want to go anyway, said it was a waste of time.

MOTHER: Working up there would have made it worse, it'll be the end of us as it is.

GWENNY: Come on now. They won't come that close to the house, will they?

MOTHER: Worrying about that and all this dreaming about America's making me ill.

GWENNY: Come and sit down here with me then.

[*Mother sits down and looks at the photos.*]

MOTHER: There's me and him there, look, on our honey-moon in Trafalgar Square, see all the pigeons.

GWENNY: He was handsome, wasn't he?

MOTHER: I'm telling you, like Errol Flynn, but here, look, wait till you see this photo.

GWENNY: Ahhh... what's that in his hair?

MOTHER: Pigeon shit, he went to stand by the fountain and a pigeon did a mess in his hair.

[Gwenny laughs.]

I thought it was funny too, but he didn't like it, he was tampin' it, he wanted to go and clean it off, but I said it was bad luck, but he wouldn't listen. He went to the gents and cleaned it off, he wouldn't listen.

GWENNY: Spoilsport wasn't he?

MOTHER: He was happy then, liked to wander he did, real wanderer.

GWENNY: What year was it?

MOTHER: Nineteen fifty-seven.

GWENNY: Was it? There's a coincidence now.

MOTHER: What was that?

GWENNY: Same year Joyce Johnson met Jack Kerouac, January, 1957.

MOTHER: This was in May, Spring wedding.

GWENNY: Same year though, mam.

MOTHER: Who are they then, I don't know them, do I?

GWENNY: I'm reading a book about them, Sid lent it to me, it's a love story.

MOTHER: They're not from round here, then?

GWENNY: No, this was in New York, it's a lovely, sad, happy story so far.

MOTHER: What's that got to do with my wedding then?

GWENNY: Well, nothing, I suppose, just a coincidence.

MOTHER: Oh, there we are then.

[Pause. They look at more photographs.]

MOTHER: That's the photo you took of Boyo when he had measles, remember?

GWENNY: Yes, he couldn't go out, and it was the summer holidays.

MOTHER: He had everything when he was small, mumps, measles, chicken pox, the lot.

GWENNY: What's he wearing sunglasses for?

MOTHER: Connection between measles and the sun, can make you blind, so you've got to wear sunglasses to protect the eyes.

[Gwenny laughs.]

GWENNY: Thin, wasn't he?

MOTHER: Lived on Jaffa Cakes and fresh air.

[Sound of someone approaching. Sid and Boyo enter.]

BOYO: Well, we've got enough wood for ten years.

MOTHER: Good news, keep the fire burning.

SID: No wood left on the trees anywhere in the country if we carry on like this.

MOTHER: Musn't forget the fire.

GWENNY: Hey, Boyo, come and have a look at these photos.

BOYO: Oh Christ, look at the state of me.

SID: Cool shades, Boyo, I don't remember you being such a cool kid.

BOYO: Stick insect, that's what I was.

MOTHER: Wouldn't eat his food.

SID: What about Gwenny here then with no front teeth?

[Laughter.]

GWENNY: Look at Sid here pulling a jib.

SID: I couldn't swim that's why, and all you buggers

were swimming.

GWENNY: What's this one here?

MOTHER: Your father giving the three of you a bath.

SID: Gwenny was only about six, look, and even then she's got two boys in the bath with her.

[Gwenny playfully pushes Sid.]

BOYO: Hey, what's Toy doing in here, in his army uniform?

GWENNY: Oh that's me that is, I had a crush on him.

BOYO: He doesn't look like that now, does he poor bugger?

[During the next short conversation, Mother moves away and switches the television on: snow.]

SID: Not his fault, he didn't like the rain, did he? Got it in his head he wanted to spend Christmas on the beach.

GWENNY: He told me he'd take me with him too.

SID: He wanted to marry you, that's why.

GWENNY: And you had a fight with him, Boyo, because of it.

BOYO: No, that wasn't the reason.

GWENNY: It was, you didn't want me to marry him.

BOYO: You were only sixteen, that's why.

SID: "She was only sixteen, only sixteen, and I was too young to knowwwww...."

BOYO: Take a day off will you, Sid, don't be a bastard all your life.

[Laughter. Boyo gets up and goes to the TV. He notices that the TV is off channel.]

BOYO: Has the telly broken down then?

MOTHER: No.

BOYO: The reception's bad, innit?

MOTHER: It's all right for me.

BOYO: There's no picture on it.

MOTHER: I've seen enough pictures for one night.

BOYO: Let me adjust it.

MOTHER: No.

BOYO: It's getting on my nerves, you can't sit there and watch something like that.

MOTHER: I said no, leave it alone.

[Boyo can only give her an exasperated look.]

SID: "Home in Missoula, home in truckee, home in Opelousas ain't no home for me...."

GWENNY: Home in old Medora...

SID: Home in Wounded Knee.

GWENNY: Home in... what is it?

SID: Ogallalla.

GWENNY: That's it.

SID: Home I'll never be.

[Laughter.]

That's my Joycey.

BOYO: What did you say?

MOTHER: He called her Joyce.

[Laughter.]

BOYO: C'mon, mun, what's the joke, who's Joyce?

GWENNY: Joyce Johnson, Jack Kerouac's girlfriend, you know.

BOYO: No.

GWENNY: She was his girlfriend.

[*Sid puts his arm round Gwenny playfully.*]

They sang that song together.

BOYO: Yeah?

SID: Yeah, good song.

GWENNY: From this book, Boyo.

[*She shows him 'On The Road'.*]

BOYO: What's so special about that, then?

[*Mother turns the volume up on the TV. Sid shouts over it, making a point.*]

SID: It's more than a book, brother, it's a way of life.

GWENNY: Mam, turn it down a bit, we can't hear.

[*Starts reading from the book.*]

"I got on the Washington bus, wasted some time there wandering around, went out of my way to see the Blue Ridge, heard the bird of Shenandoah and visited Stonewall Jackson's grave; at dusk stood in the Kanawha river, the dark and mysterious Ohio and Cincinnati at dawn then Indiana fields again, and at St. Louis...."

[*Mother suddenly gets up from the chair, walks towards Sid and spanks him.*]

SID: What the....

[*Laughter.*]

BOYO: Hey mun, mam, c'mon.

MOTHER: Don't laugh at your brother, they were laughing at you, can't you hear them?

BOYO: Just forget it.

SID: Don't ever do that again, mam.

GWENNY: There wasn't any need to do that.

MOTHER: You were laughing.

SID: So what, is there a law against laughing here?

BOYO: Come and sit down here.

SID: What the hell's wrong with her? We were only having a sing song and a read, I tell you that was out of order.

GWENNY: Forget it, she didn't mean it.

[Boyo turns off the set.]

MOTHER: I was listening to that.

[She switches it back on.]

GWENNY: Turn it off, mam, please.

MOTHER: No, it's the only company I've got here... me and Mr Snow. Some people call him interference, but he's Mr Snow, we get on like a house on fire. I get up in the morning and say hello to Mr Snow, and then before he's got time to answer I turn him off.

[She switches it off. Silence.]

He's the only friend I've got in this house. He was born when the crane blocked the signal. Hey, you're not listening to me.

SID: You're rambling again.

MOTHER: That's what you call it, is it? I tell you, I've told Mr Snow everything, all my secrets... he's good like that, I've told him everything I can't tell my own kids... keeps me company, and we all need company. You listening, Sid Lewis? Gwenny? You understand what I'm saying, all the secrets, but there's nothing funny going on between us... not like some things I see, he knows more about this house than you do, Boyo, like I wouldn't like to say there's anything funny going on between Sid and

54

Gwenny, I mean they're brother and sister, but Joyce and Jack, they're different.

SID: What are you trying to say?

MOTHER: They were lovers, see Boyo, Jack and Joyce... in love, that's all I'm saying.

GWENNY: I never thought you'd ever say something like that, mam. I never thought there'd come a day.

BOYO: C'mon, mam, you don't know what you're saying now.

MOTHER: Oh yes I do.

SID: I'm not listening to this crap any more, I'm off.

MOTHER: Don't bother, Sid... what you looking at me like that for — all of you, can't wait to get me out of the house, well don't worry, I'm going, I'm going to pack.

BOYO: Pack?

GWENNY: Where do you think you're going to go?

MOTHER: Haven't thought about it, but it's getting too hot for me in this house I can tell you.

BOYO: Hey, mam, Sid knows you didn't mean it, don't you, Sid?

SID: Yeah....

MOTHER: Oh, I do though, and I'll do it again.

SID: *You're not going to do it again, don't worry.*

MOTHER: Not safe for me in this house any more. I know you want me out of the house. Somebody's been painting my room blue, so it shows everything up in the world.

SID: Here we go again.

GWENNY: We've told you, mam, it's always been blue.

MOTHER: Painting my room that colour's the last straw. I'm out, and those cranes, driving me funny, can't fool me. I know the truth, I can't... I can't...

[She breaks down. Gwenny tries to comfort her.]

GWENNY: C'mon, mam, I'll make some tea.

MOTHER: I'm going, I'm going.

[Gwenny leads her away. They exit.]

SID: Phone the doctor, she's got to see a doctor, Boyo.

BOYO: No. He'll say she'll have to go in the mental to recover, nervous breakdown it is, and she doesn't want to go out of the house, you know how she is.

SID: We can't help her, Boyo, she's getting worse, I tell you she needs a doctor, and I'm going to phone him.

[Pause.]

BOYO: I suppose we'll have to, but she's not going unless she definitely has to.

[Sid exits. Boyo looks around resignedly. Lights fade to blackout.]

[Fade in loud opera music, Maria Callas singing an aria perhaps, as the red light of a fire builds, revealing Mother burning clothes. Boyo enters in his pants, half asleep.]

BOYO: What you burning, mam?

MOTHER: Oh, Boyo, nothing, just seeing to the fire.

BOYO: You know what time it is?

MOTHER: No, I was too busy.

BOYO: Come away from the fire. You trying to burn us to death or what?

[Sid enters, also in his pants.]

SID: There's nothing on the walls, mam, only paint. Oh Boyo, you heard the commotion as well, did you?

BOYO: What's going on then?

MOTHER: Just burning some old clothes, your father's clothes, see?

BOYO: Oh, Christ, they're my clothes, mun, what the hell mun, mam, give them here.

SID: Thought I recognised them. [laughs]

BOYO: Don't laugh, mun.

SID: Mam's been doing a bit of painting, see, Boyo, red. She's got paint everywhere.

BOYO: Half my clothes are in the fire.

MOTHER: I've got paint on my clothes too.

SID: I can tell you why she's been doing it too.

MOTHER: I couldn't help it.

SID: It's all right... ssshhh....

BOYO: Why, mam?

SID: She says there was blood on the walls.

MOTHER: Not thinks, knows. I couldn't get it off. It was getting on my nerves.

SID: She says it's dad's blood.

MOTHER: It is his blood, the cat's out of the bag now.

SID: I don't know any more, that's all she told me.

MOTHER: They're going to take me away, Boyo, but you said no matter what I'd done you'd always love me, and if something happens to me you've got to stick together, you hear me?

BOYO: All right, mam, it's all right. How about getting you back to bed now though, uh?

MOTHER: No, not in there.

SID: How did the blood get there then, mam?

MOTHER: Because I killed him.

[Silence. Mother begins to laugh hysterically. Sid and Boyo watch mesmerised. She eventually stops. Silence.]

MOTHER: The cat... is... out... of the bag.

BOYO: All right, mam, it's all right.

[Silence.]

MOTHER: What have I said?

SID: You said you felt like sleeping.

MOTHER: Did I? I do too.

BOYO: Are you ready to go to bed, mam?

MOTHER: Yes, I'm tired now, bed is best.

SID: C'mon, I'll give you a hand.

MOTHER: No, no, I can manage on my own, but I'll go to your room, my room gives me nightmares.

BOYO: You sure you can go on your own?

MOTHER: Course I can, I'm not old, and I'm still your mother.

[They watch her as she exits.]

BOYO: Fucking hell.

SID: Had a nightmare she has, that's all. Her mind playing tricks with her.

BOYO: Is that what you think?

SID: Course it is, you don't believe her, do you?

BOYO: I don't know what to believe, Sid.

SID: Everybody knows he's in America, you ask anybody. She never killed him, she probably wished she did, and now that she's ill she thinks she has done, got it all mixed up in her head, that's all.

BOYO: I tell you, I don't know whether I'm coming or going, too much for me this is.

SID: Don't let it get to you, brother, it's all in her mind, believe me, she's telling lies, it's in her head.

BOYO: How come we haven't heard a word from him since he went then?

SID: Because he probably thinks it's the only way. I bet you he's laying plans now for us to go over there on a visit. That's my opinion anyway.

BOYO: How can you be that sure, Sid?

SID: I know, mun, I've got a feeling about it, I believe that's all, if I didn't look at it that way I'd go nuts.

[Pause.]

BOYO: No point in saying anything to Gwenny.

SID: No, it'll make her worry, confuse her, best thing to do is forget about it, and hope she gets better. Goodnight, I'm off to bed.

BOYO: Goodnight.

[Sid exits. Boyo stands, looks through photo album. Music plays softly to blackout.]

Act Three

['Riders On The Storm' plays in blackout. Lights up on Sid doing well with the card trick on the table. Boyo doing press-ups on the floor. Music fades out.]

SID: Oi... Boyo, what you reckon to this masterpiece then?

BOYO: That's all right innit, how did you get that far then?

SID: Solid foundation, Boyo. Everything Sid Lewis builds is solid. Skill too — two of them together, fatal combination, mate.

BOYO: No flies on you see, are there, brother?

SID: No, and the odd ones I do find flying around my head either went to Oxford or Cambridge.

BOYO: On a day trip.

SID: No, Boyo, only because of their brains, Boyo, only 'cos of their brains.

[Gwenny enters.]

GWENNY: Never guess what I've just seen.

[Gwenny stands still in the middle of the room.]

I was walking down the street right, and it's raining, the clouds were low, and in front of me is someone walking a dog, it's a chihuahua.

[Pause.]

Then I hear this bus coming down the road behind me, a big red bus like a school bus, and it passes me, whoosh, like that, and it's just about to pass the dog, who's on a lead, when the dog strays into the road, and gets squashed flat, and the owner's still holding onto the lead, just staring at the squashed dog. And all of a sudden I feel like laughing, not just a giggle, but a hysterical one.

[Pause.]

SID: Yeah, what it is right, is that somewhere deep down inside, you just hate chihuahuas.

GWENNY: Why? Then I go and see if I can help. The man's just staring down, I feel sorry for him now. Then he turns round and says "I've only just given him a whole tin of chum, and now the poor bugger's gone and got squashed". Then I asked him what the dog's name was and he turns round and says "Jack".

SID: Kerouac.

GWENNY: That's what I said, and he says "Who's that?" and I say "He's an American who wrote books." So the two of us stand there, looking at this American novelist who's squashed on the road, and you know what?

SID: What?

GWENNY: I haven't thought of an ending to it yet.

[She squeals in victory.]

BOYO: Oh, Christ mun, Gwenny.

SID: Hey come on, Gwenny, give us the ending, got to be an ending.

GWENNY: And the girl turned to her brother and said I made it all up. I was dreaming. I've never even seen a chihuahua, and what's more, I haven't been out of the house either. I've been in my room reading, and trying on clothes.

[She looks at them and they all laugh. Sudden loud crash of industry offstage.]

BOYO: Jesus, are they blowing up the world or what?

[Goes to the window.]

SID: Fuck 'em. I've got a masterpiece going here. Hey, seen my cards, Gwenny?

BOYO: You can see the top of the cranes now, look.

GWENNY: They'll eat the house one day.

SID: Let's go up and have a look.

GWENNY: What now?

SID: Yeah, come on.

GWENNY: You coming, Boyo?

BOYO: No. I'll stay here and guard the house.

SID: Come on then....

[Sid gets up and accidentally tumbles the cards. We see that Sid has glued his card trick together.]

Shit.

BOYO: Ah... look, Gwenny, look. That's why his card trick works... he's glued them all together! *[holding up the card trick]*

GWENNY: That's cheating, Sid.

BOYO: Yeah....

SID: Well it just goes to show, see brother, don't believe all you see.

BOYO: Yeah, I'll remember that.

SID: C'mon, Gwenny, let's go.

[Sid and Gwenny exit. Lights change and come up on the Open Cast mine. A labourer appears with a shovel. Sid and Gwenny enter.]

SID: See that bloke over there, Gwenny?

GWENNY: Yeah.

SID: He's a labourer, he got the job me and Boyo should have had.

GWENNY: What's he laughing for?

SID: He's not laughing, he's grunting.

GWENNY: Looks as if he's lost something.

SID: Come on, let's go and ask him.

[They walk towards the labourer who's staring at the floor and leaning on his shovel.]

SID: All right?

LAB: Uh... yeah.

SID: What's happening then?

LAB: Do you work here?

SID: No, we live in the house down there.

GWENNY: All the blasting is affecting our house, every blast shakes it.

LAB: Nothing to do with me, go and tell the gaffer.

SID: Where's he?

LAB: In the shed on the top there, but I wouldn't bother.

SID: Why not?

LAB: He died.

GWENNY: Uh?

LAB: Dead head he is, you got time for a chat?

SID: Yeah, but....

LAB: Don't worry about him, they give him bacon sandwiches and he's right, don't have a chance to talk here see.

GWENNY: What you looking for then?

LAB: I'm not looking for nothing, given up that crack.

SID: What's on the floor then?

LAB: Oh, I've lost something.

SID: What have you lost?

[The Labourer looks at him.]

LAB: What kind of question's that, wus?

SID: We saw you looking at the floor. You said you've lost something.

GWENNY: We'll help you find it.

LAB: I don't want to find it, it'll upset me. I've lost it I know, but that doesn't mean I want to find it, does it? And you can't find something you're not looking for.

SID: I tried for this job see, me and my brother. I....

LAB: Here, you can have a go if you want.

SID: What you have to do?

LAB: Nothing or everything, does your head in.

GWENNY: How do you mean?

LAB: We're standing on coal, innit? That machine over there is, and that lorry is. The machine fills the lorry with coal, and my job is to throw the bits of coal that tip over back on the lorry, you got me? But the trick is, how can you tell which bits fell off the lorry, 'cos it all looks the same, don't it? So you either shovel everything you see back in the lorry, or you don't bother.

SID: And you don't bother.

LAB: No, my head's gone. Hey mind your heads, the driver's stoned out of his box. The bloke before him got sacked because he wouldn't get out of his cab.

He tried to drive it home, by the time he'd got there it was time to come back to work, so he's forgotten where he lives now.

GWENNY: They look like dinosaurs.

LAB: No, the dinosaur's extinct.

GWENNY: Electric dinosaurs.

LAB: If you want, yeah.

SID: Do you talk to the bloke in the cab?

LAB: Sometimes he tells me to go to the store for a long wait, so I go, and wait there all day. Best part of the job.

GWENNY: Lucky you didn't get the jobs, Sid.

[Sid nods.]

SID: What is it you've lost then?

LAB: My head.

[Gwenny laughs.]

Is it funny? *[suddenly aggressive]*

GWENNY: No, no, it's just me, laughing.

SID: How did it happen?

LAB: Things weren't going my way when I was younger. I was about eighteen and I put my head in the sand. I took it out when they gave me this job, but when I looked in the mirror, I didn't recognize the face looking back at me see. This new face was different to the one I put in the sand.

SID: How do you mean?

LAB: Well, the old face for a start was younger, but that's nothing, the old face had clear eyes, the mouth used to laugh and talk about plans for the rest of the body, and the brain used to dream a lot, you follow me?

SID: What's wrong with the new face?

LAB: The new face is different, the eyes have lost their shine, the skin is sagging, the teeth are rotting, the hair is turning grey, the plans have got dust on them, and the dreams have just fallen out of the ears, can you see? That's why I reckon I must have lost it, came off when I wasn't looking, and all those things happened because it's been kicked about on the floor, like lorries gone over it.

GWENNY: Dinosaurs eaten it.

LAB: Yeah, sheep pissed on it, slug trails all over the brain and cobwebs in the memory.

SID: Hey listen, mate, you've got to find it, I'll give you a hand.

LAB: Is there something wrong with you?

GWENNY: He wants to help.

LAB: That head's lost for good, this is the one I'm stuck with now. I just wish I hadn't put it in the sand in the first place, I might not have lost it, 'cos I know in my bones I've lost something, gives me an ache in my guts. I don't want to find it now, it's too late, it's too fucking late.

                [Pause.]

SID: That won't happen to me.

LAB: You reckon?

SID: Yeah, I'm off I am.

LAB: Where you going?

SID: Going to America we are, me and my sister here.

LAB: I've got to go now, see the machine's started walking, got to follow the machine.

GWENNY: We'll come again if you want.

LAB: Yeah, come if you want.

GWENNY: What's your name?

LAB: Oh, I don't know, make one up.

GWENNY: You've got to have a name.

LAB: Clint.

GWENNY: My name's Gwenny, and this is my brother, Si....

SID: Jack.

[*Gwenny looks at him.*]

Jack Kerouac.

LAB: Clint Eastwood, I'm the man with no name.

[*The Labourer laughs and walks away.*]

GWENNY: What did you want to say that for?

SID: I don't know, for a laugh.

GWENNY: I'm not coming up here again, something crazy about it.

SID: I know what he's saying though, do you?

[*Gwenny nods.*]

GWENNY: C'mon, I want to go.

SID: You go, I'll follow you down now.

[*Gwenny exits. Sid is looking out. Sound of industry increases. Sound of wind and screaming.*]

SID: Sid Lewis, R.I.P.

[*Sid walks away.*]

[*Lights up on Mother in a hospital room. Boyo enters.*]

BOYO: Hello, mam?

MOTHER: Yes Jesus, it's me, Mrs Lewis.

BOYO: No, mam, it's me, Boyo.

[Mother looks around.]

MOTHER: Oh, I thought you were Jesus.

[Pause.]

BOYO: I brought you some fruit.

MOTHER: Oh, put them over there.

[Boyo puts them down.]

BOYO: Not a bad room, mam.

MOTHER: What do you want here?

BOYO: Came to see you that's all.

MOTHER: How's the house?

BOYO: All right.

[Pause.]

BOYO: Gwenny keeps writing him letters to America.

MOTHER: You'll have to tell her to stop.

BOYO: I've been reading them.

MOTHER: I've told you already, he's not there.

BOYO: I don't want to upset her. They're calling her Miss America.

MOTHER: Who is?

BOYO: The Post Office. The woman told me she comes in every week to see if there's a letter.

MOTHER: What fruit did you bring?

BOYO: Apples, do you want one?

[Mother takes an apple.]

Did you give her an address, mam?

MOTHER: I can't remember.

BOYO: Sid told me you gave it to her.

MOTHER: She was pestering me.

BOYO: So you did then?

MOTHER: Yes.

BOYO: So he is in America?

MOTHER: An address doesn't mean anything.

BOYO: What's the address then?

[Silence.]

Mam?

MOTHER: Mr Clem Lewis, Main Street, Dodge City, The West, America.

[She laughs.]

BOYO: Is that what you've given Gwenny?

[Laughter.]

Is it?

[Mother laughs.]

BOYO: She must know it's wrong, she can't believe that.

MOTHER: You better ask her, she's the one sending the letters. Me and Mr Snow were sitting there one day and there was a Western on, and I turned round to Gwenny and said that's where he'll be. But you know what the worst of it is, he didn't have to bother to think of going to America, and you tell Sid and Gwenny not to waste their money. Somebody in here told me you don't have to go to the Wild West to find America, they've built a Wild West up the valley — you can go there and be a cowboy for a day. You can dress in your cowboy outfit, have a drink in the saloon, and they've got Country and Western singers every Friday and Saturday night. If your father had only waited a bit, he'd still be here. The bloke who told me is a cowboy, he thinks he's a cowboy anyway.

[She laughs. Pause.]

BOYO: I'm going now, mam.

MOTHER: To guard the house. I think I'm lucky to be in here, nobody'll hurt me in here. I hear you can see the Open Cast from the window now.

[Boyo nods.]

MOTHER: They're coming nearer, won't be long now.

BOYO: I love Gwenny, mam, and I don't want to lie to her.

MOTHER: Then tell her the truth.

BOYO: I don't know what it is.

MOTHER: You still don't believe me, do you?

[Lights change. Fade up Lou Reed's 'Walk On The Wild Side'. Sid is reading to Gwenny, Boyo sits at the table, annoyed.]

SID: "I'm with you in Rockland, where we hug and kiss the United States under our bedsheets, the United States that coughs all night and won't let us sleep."

[Pause.]

"Where we wake up electrified out of the coma by our own souls, airplanes roaring over the roof, they've come to drop angelic bombs, the hospital illuminates itself, imaginary walls collapse, victory, forget you're underwater, we're free in my dreams, you walk dripping from a sea journey on the highway across America in tears to the door of my cottage in the Western night."

BOYO: What in fuck's name are you talking about, Sid?

SID: Freedom, brother, escape.

GWENNY: Do you think Joyce Johnson's pretty, Sid?

[During the following dialogue Boyo finds a bottle of

pills on the table which Gwenny nonchalantly takes away from him.]

SID: Yeah.

GWENNY: She wore nice clothes, nobody I know dresses like that.

SID: Fifties wasn't it?

GWENNY: Where's the Upper West Side?

SID: New York.

GWENNY: Greenwich Village?

SID: That's where she met Jack.

BOYO: You finished that book then?

SID: Yeah, ages ago, Gwenny's read it too, do you want to borrow it?

BOYO: No, I'm all right.

GWENNY: "Putting on a pair of copper earrings en route to Jack...."

[Gwenny looks in the mirror, puts on earrings.]

Do you like these, Sid?

[Sid nods.]

SID: You could look as pretty as her, Gwen.

GWENNY: Think so?

SID: No trouble.

GWENNY: Even without the copper earrings?

SID: They don't have to be copper, just big and round.

GWENNY: And then a black skirt, jumper.

SID: And black stockings. I could call you Joyce.

GWENNY: And then all you need is a pair of faded old jeans and like a lumberjack shirt and I could call you

Jack.

SID: You could be my girlfriend.

GWENNY: And Boyo, you can be Allen Ginsberg or some-body.

BOYO: It's all right. I'll stick to being Boyo.

[Gwenny pulls a face at him behind his back.]

SID: It was him that introduced Jack to Joyce.

BOYO: Oh great, mun.

GWENNY: It was a love story see, Boyo.

BOYO: How long am I going to have to listen to this crap?

GWENNY: Don't be like that.

BOYO: Well Christ, mun, it's the same old crack every day, Jack this, Joyce that, why don't you give it a rest.

SID: Read the book, then you can join in.

BOYO: I don't want to read the book, I'm not interested, you're like a pair of kids, mun, playing.

GWENNY: Nothing wrong with that, is there?

BOYO: I'm not saying that but it's all this yankage, give it a rest for Christ sake.

GWENNY: Oh, poor Boyo, he feels left out, Jack.

[She smooths his hair.]

BOYO: Get off mun, Gwenny.

SID: Stop feeling sorry for yourself, Boyo.

BOYO: I'm not, but I'm sick to death with all this fucking dreaming about America. If you don't like it here, why don't you just fuck off out of here on the first plane?

SID: If I had the money, Boyo, I'd be long gone.

BOYO: The sooner the better, and you're just as bad, Gwen, all these letters.

GWENNY: How do you know I've been writing letters?

BOYO: Mam told me, and she showed me his address too.

GWENNY: So.

BOYO: Well, it's false, innit? She made it up.

GWENNY: How do you know?

BOYO: Well it's obvious, innit? There's no number or nothing, and she got it out of a Western — Dodge City, The West.

GWENNY: I don't care, he'll get it somehow.

BOYO: Don't be so soft, mun, there's millions of Lewis's in America.

GWENNY: I don't care what you say, it won't stop me, and at least we'll have somewhere to go, when the Open Cast takes over the house.

BOYO: It's not going to take over the house.

SID: Course it is, coming nearer every day, before long they'll be knocking on the door saying "Oi, we want your house," and you'll say, "You can't have it, it's part of a street," and they'll turn around and say, "We know, but we own the street," and then where will you be?

GWENNY: Everybody'll go in the end, Boyo, there's nothing here for us any more, it's a forgotten town. You've got to think ahead, keep your options open.

BOYO: Think it's as easy as that do you? Just clear off. Well, I don't know about you, but this is where I belong, and I'm staying, no fucking tinpot dreaming for me.

SID: You know what's wrong with you, you've got your head in the sand, and I know what happens to

73

people like that.

BOYO: Mam told us we had to stick together, and she's right.

SID: Mam's lost her marbles, or haven't you noticed? Got to change and swing with the crack, and I'm making plans for it. The only ones for me are the ones who burn, got me, Boyo?

BOYO: Like a planet is it, Gwenny?

[Boyo looks disgusted. Lights change. Sid and Gwenny drink bourbon and swallow pills as Lou Reed's 'New York' album plays.]

SID: Girl met boy on a blind date arranged by Allen Ginsberg, it was January, 1957.

GWENNY: The girl was Joyce Johnson.

SID: The boy was Jack Kerouac.

GWENNY: You can be Allen Ginsberg, Boyo.

[Boyo enters.]

BOYO: What you playing?

GWENNY: Playing out a love story.

BOYO: Who the hell is Allen Ginsberg?

SID: He's a poet.

GWENNY: He introduced the two lovers.

BOYO: This is Jack, and this is Joyce, how's that?

SID: Help yourself to the Jack Daniels, Joyce.

BOYO: And don't tell me he's a baseball player.

SID: Wrong — it's a whisky.

BOYO: Well, Jack, did you find your American dream?

GWENNY: That's not a fair question, Boyo.

BOYO: Why not?

SID: No, I went half mad in 1967, and died in my mother's arms.

BOYO: Not much of a dream then is it?

GWENNY: If you're not going to play the game properly, there's no point in playing.

BOYO: Forget your bastard games, I'm going down the pub to get pissed.

          [He exits.]

SID: Care for a dance, Joyce?

GWENNY: Sure, Jack.

          [Presley's 'Love Me Tender' comes on, and there is something strangely sexual about the dance. While this goes on Boyo knocks back the booze, in another part of the stage. The dance comes to an end, and Boyo staggers in, drunk. Gwenny is leaning on Sid's shoulder, music low in background.]

BOYO: The lovers still on their feet, and I've got a poem for them, a Boyo poem, want to hear it? Any minute now, a cup of tea is going to come in here, sit down, watch me light a cigarette, and as the smoke and steam rise it's going to get slowly, contentedly... drunk.

          [Boyo tries to join in, and the atmosphere changes.]

GWENNY: Get off, Boyo, will you, spoilt it all now.

          [Gwenny walks away.]

BOYO: Hey, where you going, come back I haven't finished yet, we've....

          [Gwenny exits.]

SID: Sit down, before you fall down, shit for brains.

BOYO: Got to stick together, mun, oi, don't go to bed now mun, I'm a bit pissed, that's all.

SID: Thanks, mate, thanks a lot.

BOYO: Cat and the boys were asking after you, Sid... if you can't bring... hic... Mohammed to the mountain, take the mountain to, him... or something.

            [Sid exits.]

            I drink coke, eat popcorn, wear baseball hats, watch the films, but all I'm asking what... who the fuck is Jack Kerouac, and these books? A book is a book, Bill and Ben the flower pot men, I remember that book... stay and have a drink with your brother... I've got the cans, got the chips. Have a chip, have a kip — it's a poem, Allen Ginsberg, eat your heart out, pal.

            [Falls over.]

            I'm confused I am, always confusion, messy, have a drink... somebody turn the light out.

            [Blackout. Discordant music plays. Lights up on Mother, wearing a Welsh hat and daffodil. Boyo is dreaming.]

MOTHER: Boyo! Sid? Gwenny?

            [Silence.]

BOYO: Where's the wind coming from?

            [Silence.]

            Sid? Gwenny?

MOTHER: It's not Gwenny, it's me.

BOYO: Mam, what the hell are you doing here?

MOTHER: I live here.

BOYO: How did you get out of the hospital?

MOTHER: This is the hospital.

BOYO: What you got that hat on for?

MOTHER: It's only a hat, did you think I'd walk in here with no hat on or what?

BOYO: I'll have to take you back to the hospital now.

MOTHER: Don't talk rubbish, this is the hospital.

[Boyo looks at her.]

BOYO: Christ, it's freezing in here.

MOTHER: You let the fire go out, that's why.

BOYO: It wasn't my fault, I've been out all night. Gwenny was here, she should have been looking after the fire.

MOTHER: You like your drink, don't you?

BOYO: I'm not going to argue, mam. I'll go and get Gwenny.

MOTHER: What you mean, go and get Gwenny?

BOYO: She's upstairs, sleeping.

MOTHER: There's no upstairs here.

[Boyo stares at her.]

You go and have a look.

[Boyo picks up the candle and wanders around.]

BOYO: Where the hell's this, where the hell am I?

MOTHER: In the hospital, where do you think you are?

BOYO: I must have fallen asleep in the house, how the hell did I get here and where's Gwenny... and Sid?

MOTHER: Gone.

BOYO: What do you mean, mam, gone, what gone?

MOTHER: Gone away.

[Mother exits. Boyo runs around shouting and screaming, cacophony of discordant noise and percussion. He collapses. Blackout. Then Gwenny appears in her dressing gown. Lights up.]

GWENNY: Boyo, wake up.

> *[Gwenny shakes him gently and he wearily opens his eyes. On seeing her he shoots back in reaction.]*

BOYO: Get away from me, get away from me.

GWENNY: Sssh... Boyo, it's all right, it's me.

> *[Boyo stares hard at her and looks around, slowly getting his bearings.]*

GWENNY: You must have had a nightmare, you've been ranting and raving. You woke me up.

> *[He continues to stare at her.]*

GWENNY: It's all right now.

BOYO: What time is it?

GWENNY: Time to go to bed, it's late.

BOYO: Where's everybody gone? Mam was here and Sid.

GWENNY: All in bed, that's where you should be.

> *[Boyo holds his head in his hands.]*

GWENNY: You drank too much. All right now?

BOYO: My head's like a bucket. *[nods]* It's all right now, you go to bed.

> *[Gwenny looks at him.]*

GWENNY: See you tomorrow.

BOYO: Gwenny.

GWENNY: What?

BOYO: Where's Sid?

GWENNY: Sleeping, where do you think he is?

> *[Gwenny exits. Boyo lights a cigarette and thinks. Lights change. Exterior house. Sid is chopping wood with an axe. Boyo is sick in a corner.]*

SID: How's your head?

BOYO: Coming off, and my mouth's as dry as an Arab's dap.

SID: What time did you get to bed in the end?

BOYO: I don't know — late.

SID: See anybody you knew in the pub?

BOYO: A few, they were asking after you.

          [Pause.]

          Where did you sleep last night?

SID: In the bed, where do you think I slept?

BOYO: You weren't in there this morning when I looked in.

SID: I was in Gwenny's bed that's why. She got a bit tight last night as well. I had to carry her to bed, she fell asleep down here, and I took her up, and I fell asleep there too.

BOYO: Looked all right to me, she heard me, I was having bad dreams, she came to see if I was all right.

SID: What you trying to say?

BOYO: I wanted to know.

SID: Yeah, but I can see what you're thinking, and I don't like it.

BOYO: When I saw you last night, dancing — I don't know, it didn't look right.

SID: Gwenny's my sister for fuck sake.

BOYO: I saw the way you were looking at her.

SID: You'd better watch what you're saying, mate.

          [Facing up to Boyo.]

BOYO: Lay off, Sid, I was only asking.

SID: You better take a good look at yourself, saying things like that.

BOYO: It was all the Jack and Joyce stuff.

SID: That was a game, Boyo, playing a game.

BOYO: It didn't look like a game to me, that's what I'm saying.

SID: Well you're wrong, you're talking incest for Christ sake.

          [Pause.]

BOYO: Hey, Sid, forget I said it, I'm sorry, didn't mean that.

SID: Good job you didn't tell Gwenny.

BOYO: Yeah, yeah, look I said I'm sorry, we're living on top of each other, it's getting to me that's all.

SID: We'll just forget about it, O.K.?

BOYO: Yeah, sorry.

          [Sid continues to chop wood.]

SID: I tell you what you need, Boyo, is a girlfriend, help take your mind off things.

BOYO: What about you then?

SID: Do me good too I know, but I'm not the marrying kind, see Boyo — fucking minefield if you ask me, anyway you're the one that's staying, I'll be off. But if you do get married when I'm gone and you have a Kevin or a Helen you make sure they don't grow up to pull the wings off butterflies and throw fireworks at the old age. I'll see you back in the house.

BOYO: Hey, I thought I'd call in on mam, you coming?

SID: No, I'll see you back at the house.

          [Sid exits. Lights change. Come up on Mother in the hospital wearing a Welsh hat and Daffodil. Boyo enters

80

looking dishevelled and confused.]

MOTHER: What are you looking at me like that for?

BOYO: Why you wearing those clothes?

MOTHER: You don't know then?

BOYO: Know what?

MOTHER: You've forgotten.

BOYO: Forgotten what?

MOTHER: Tell me what the date is?

BOYO: I don't know, end of February.

MOTHER: Wrong, it's March the 1st, it's St. David's Day and you've forgotten.

BOYO: And that's why you're wearing your clothes.

MOTHER: Some of us don't forget.

BOYO: I lost touch of the days, and I had this dream and you were wearing those clothes.

MOTHER: I don't want to hear your excuses.

[Pause.]

Like my daffodil?

BOYO: It's plastic.

MOTHER: Didn't have real ones, and the plastic ones stay yellow forever.

[She eats her cawl. Boyo watches. Then he walks over and looks in the bowl.]

BOYO: Cawl...?

MOTHER: Mmm... neck of lamb, I made a pot full of it. Are you hungry? You can have some if you want, it's still hot.

BOYO: There's nothing in the dish, mam.

[Pause. Mother looks into the bowl. Starts to laugh.]

MOTHER: Isn't there?

[She laughs a bit more. Suddenly she throws it to the floor.]

MOTHER: You're right, there's nothing there.

[Pause.]

You know what, I've been waiting for someone to say that to me all day. Every time the nurse or the doctor comes in here for something, I've been pretending to eat my cawl, and you know what? Not one of them has told me there's nothing in it, not one of them. Do they think I don't know that, uh? What would you say, Boyo? Don't you think I know there's no cawl in there, but do they say something? No. Because they don't want to upset me, because I'm mad, that's why. Tell me, Boyo, who's joking who here? And I'll tell you another thing, there's no Mr Snow either, in fact there's never been a Mr Snow. It's all a pack of lies.

[She sits down triumphantly in the chair.]

BOYO: How long have you been pretending then?

MOTHER: I don't know, but long enough for me to enjoy it — mad Mrs Lewis in the house of fools.

[She laughs maniacally.]

And some nights I howl like a sick dog, howl and bark here, and in they come with some tablets and ask me quietly to stop barking... me, a woman my age, barking? ...what's the world coming to? Your sister told me one day... she was scared of the dinosaurs, and then she told me not to tell you, well is that sense? ...it's not the dinosaurs she's afraid of, it's herself... doesn't know if she's coming or going, and you don't know either... you, Boyo, you... you told me yourself.

[Pause. Mother has gone silent.]

BOYO: Mam?

MOTHER: I'm still here.

BOYO: You've got to come back home.

[Silence.]

You hear what I'm saying?

[Silence.]

Say something.

[Silence.]

Don't stop now, mam, please.

[Silence.]

MOTHER: There's a gooseberry going up and down in a lift, and a baby saying boo to a bear, and your father isn't in America.

BOYO: You've got to listen to me.

MOTHER: He's not in America I said, never went, never been, never grew a kidney bean. Now go on before I start barking, visiting's over, go back to your cell.

BOYO: You've got to tell me the truth, mam, please.

MOTHER: The house is rocking I can tell.

BOYO: Things are changing, that's all. You were right, you've got to try and get better.

MOTHER: I'll never get out of here. Where have you been living? Haven't you heard the news, everybody else has heard it?

BOYO: What news?

MOTHER: On the Open Cast. Some digging dinosaur has found a body up there.

BOYO: When?

MOTHER: This morning, a man's body.

BOYO: Who is it?

MOTHER: They don't know yet, but I know, and it won't be long until they find out too.

BOYO: Who is it, mam?

[Blackout, lights up on the Open Cast. Gwenny and Sid approach the labourer we saw earlier.]

SID: Oi, Clint, who is it, do you know?

LAB: Yeah, it was me who found him, I thought it was my head in the beginning.

GWENNY: But it wasn't.

LAB: No.

SID: Who is it then, local bloke?

LAB: Bloke called... Clem Lewis. Have you heard of him?

SID: What....

LAB: They reckon he's been there fifteen years.

[Gwenny laughs hysterically.]

SID: My old man was called Clem Lewis, must be two of them, my old man is in America.

LAB: Yeah?... What's so funny then, have I said something funny?

GWENNY: You're a bad liar, that's all.

LAB: I'm not lying, they say his wife killed him.

SID: How do they know it's him?

LAB: Dental records — by his teeth. I wouldn't tell you lies. Hey, he's not your father is he?

[Gwenny runs at him hitting out. Labourer laughs maniacally at them. Lights change back to the hospital.

Boyo sits with his head in his hands. Mother takes off her hat.]

MOTHER: Your father, I killed him, but you didn't believe me — never went to America. True as there's no cawl in the bowl. I couldn't get the blood off the wall see, too much blue, should have been red, and if the Open Cast hadn't come, we'd be right. I warned you about it, I told you to be strong, to stick together, you think the house is rocking, you haven't seen nothing yet, but I tell you one thing, if you don't stand up to it, your roots are going to fly out of the ground to wherever the wind blows them.

[Silence. Mother looks at him.]

I don't want to see you again, Boyo.

[Pause.]

Kiss me goodbye, Boyo.

[She kisses him and exits. Boyo looks defeated. Lights change to the house. Sid and Gwenny crawl around drunkenly to Jim Morrison's 'American Prayer'. Boyo enters and walks aimlessly around. Music fades.]

SID: The police have been.

BOYO: For what?

SID: They've found his body, Boyo, on the mountain.

[Silence. Gwenny is sick in the corner.]

They think mam killed him. But it's the wrong bloke, couldn't have been him, could it? 'Coz he's in America.

[Sid laughs, half cries in disbelief. Lights change to a surreal court-room, where the Labourer plays the prosecuting council.]

MOTHER: I killed him, is that what you want to hear? All I know, I did it to keep us all together, under one roof, he didn't want to belong any more — if we followed him I don't know where we would have ended up, but I tell you one thing, at least my kids know who they are.

[Labourer enters with a torch.]

LAB: Don't be so soft, mun. Is your name Gwen Lewis?

GWENNY: No.

LAB: Do you know who she is?

GWENNY: No.

LAB: Where were you born?

GWENNY: On the Upper West Side, New York City.

LAB: Do you know where your father is?

[Pause.]

GWENNY: Yes, Dodge City.

LAB: And your mother?

GWENNY: There she is. She doesn't live with us any more.

LAB: Do you remember your father leaving?

GWENNY: No, I don't remember, I don't remember, I don't want to remember.

[Light on Sid.]

LAB: What do you remember, mate?

SID: Are you talking to me? I can't remember, I mean it was a long time ago, but murder is murder, that's all I have to say.

[Labourer laughs and exits.]

BOYO: He bought me a horse for Christmas, a toy plastic horse, I was playing with it in front of the fire, there was a lot of shouting and I was told to go upstairs. I stayed there for a long time, but then I went downstairs. The fire had gone out, and there was nobody there. I picked up my horse but my fingers went straight through him, he'd melted by the fire, and his feet were stuck to the carpet, all the way from Hong Kong to melt on the carpet in my house. Then my mother came in and told me our father had gone to America. That's all.

MOTHER: All I know is that I've done my best, lie it might have been, but the truth hurts. If they turn out to be flotsam and I'm the mother of flotsam, at least I know I loved them, you hear me? I loved them, that's all I've got to say.

[Mother slowly walks into the darkness. Blackout. Lights up in the house. It is a mess, strewn with cans and bottles. Boyo sits staring blankly at a TV set covered in snow. Sid and Gwenny carry on oblivious, on a cocktail of drink and drugs.]

GWENNY: They found the wrong man on the mountain, didn't they, Jack? It must have been the wrong man because he didn't have a face.

SID: And there were worms in his head.

GWENNY: And snails in his heart. Couldn't have been dad, Jack, it couldn't have been, they made it up to make us feel bad.

SID: It was the wrong man, baby, they found the wrong man.

GWENNY: Because you knew him, didn't you?

SID: Yeah, me and him had some crazy times.

GWENNY: Clem Lewis from Dodge City.

SID: Yeah, Clem from Dodge. Stayed with him when we were 'On The Road', came looking for the dream with us, used to talk about his Joycey all the time. He said, "I know a girl on the other side of heaven, you've got to meet her, Jack," that's what he used to say. He said, "You'll love her, she'll take

87

you to dreamworld."

[Gwenny giggles.]

GWENNY: Was he a good man, Jack?

SID: The best, the best.

GWENNY: Then he can't be dead, can he?

SID: Clem Lewis will never die, Joyce, never, ever.

GWENNY: So we can be happy in the house of America, Jack.

SID: Yeah... everything's fine, as we roll along this way. I am positive beyond doubt that everything will be taken care of. The thing will go along itself, and we won't go off the road, and I can sleep.

GWENNY: It's beautiful, Jack... kiss me.

[They kiss.]

In the heart of America with my baby Jack.

BOYO: Leave her alone, Sid.

SID: C'mon, man, I can't tell if you're dead or alive. You've got to open your eyes, brother, you've got to let things swing. Nothing stays the same forever, get on the world's car and never get off, hitch a ride to the other side of the sun, c'mon, can't you smell the space of Iowa on the mountains, see Manhattan on TV and on our streets, play pool with a man who's seen the Chicago Bears. The world gets bigger as it gets smaller, the summer's come, brother.

GWENNY: Put this hat on.

[Gwenny gives Boyo a baseball hat.]

BOYO: Get away from me, can't you see I'm busy?

GWENNY: That's not the way it's supposed to be, you've got it on back to front.

BOYO: What is it?

GWENNY: It's a baseball hat.

BOYO: You don't play baseball, do you?

SID: You don't have to play baseball to wear the hat, man.

BOYO: Get it off, it's not my size.

GWENNY: But it suits you, it suits you.

BOYO: It's not my size, I said.

GWENNY: You can adjust it, it'll fit anybody's head, see?

BOYO: Take it back, I'm busy.

GWENNY: Don't be a spoilsport. Look there's a mirror, have a look in the mirror.

BOYO: If you don't take it, I'll throw it.

GWENNY: You could wear it anywhere.

[Boyo scrunches it and throws it to the floor, and spits. Fade up 'Do You Know The Way To San Jose' low. Boyo exits.]

GWENNY: There wasn't any need to do that. He spat on the floor too.

SID: If he doesn't want to play, we can't help him. Just think, when the sun goes down and I sit watching the long long skies over New Jersey, and sense all that raw land that rolls in one huge bulge over the West Coast.

GWENNY: And I'm sitting at the table in the exact centre of the universe, with some bourbon and my Jack talking about living and dying and freedom. Make me happy, Jack.

[Laughter.]

SID: Are you wearing the black stockings, Joyce?

[She nods.]

I like black stockings on virgins, Joyce.

GWENNY: Make me happy, Jack.

SID: When will I get to feel them, baby?

GWENNY: When you tell me I love you.

SID: I love you, I want to feel your skin like ripe earth.

GWENNY: Will you marry me, Jack?

SID: Yeah, when will it be?

GWENNY: Now, now, there's no time like now.

SID: I could eat you, Joycey.

GWENNY: Then eat me, lover.

SID: All good things take time.

GWENNY: Are you really Jack Kerouac?

SID: Look in my face, can you see the truth in my face?

[Gwenny looks and nods.]

Feel.

GWENNY: I love you, Jack.

[They kiss. Boyo enters and watches.]

BOYO: Leave her alone, Sid.

GWENNY: Who's that?

SID: Nothing, nobody.

GWENNY: Come and make us a baby, Jack, a sweet pea dream baby that runs in the Florida sun in winter, sleeps all night and smiles all day: a baby to be proud of, a baby to sing and dance and fly in the air. Come and roll over me and write poems on my belly. How many b's in baby? I love you, I love you.

[Sid and Gwenny undress and make love in front of a red fire as music plays. Boyo watches for a while then exits. He returns with a club. Suddenly he attacks.]

BOYO: Leave her alone, you bastard.

[A violent fight ensues, ending with all the furniture and props re-arranged. It ends with Gwenny smashing a bottle over Boyo's head. Sid and Gwenny exit. Blackout. Silence. Lights up slowly on Boyo, sitting in a pool of light, smoking.]

BOYO: There is... a house... in New Orleans... they call... the rising sun... Jack Kerouac... Joyce Johnson... Allen Ginsberg... No Allen.

[Lights up in house. Gwenny sits alone.]

BOYO: Gwenny?

GWENNY: You talking to me?

BOYO: It's me, Gwenny, Boyo.

GWENNY: I don't know you.

BOYO: You all right?

GWENNY: I've got morning sickness.

BOYO: We've got to get out of the house, Gwenny.

GWENNY: Stop calling me that.

BOYO: Come with me, we've got to get out, come on.

GWENNY: I know you, you're the spoilsport.

BOYO: Come on you need some air, come for a walk with me.

GWENNY: I don't walk with strangers.

BOYO: Give me your hand.

GWENNY: Don't touch me.

[Pause.]

You want to take my baby from me, don't you?

BOYO: Baby?

GWENNY: We're going to have a baby, me and Jack.

BOYO: He's your brother.

GWENNY: Don't try and fool me whoever you are. If you want to leave the house, you go, but we're staying here.

BOYO: I don't believe you.

GWENNY: We're thinking of calling the baby Dodge, what do you think?

BOYO: I don't, Gwenny.

[Boyo exits. Fade up Patti Smith's 'Because The Night' as Sid enters the house. He looks at Gwenny. There is a long silence.]

GWENNY: I'm going to have a baby, Jack.

SID: Oh yeah? Big or small, or medium, how would you like it done, madam?

GWENNY: It's true, Jack, a love baby... I can feel it... a love baby.

SID: Any chance of coffee?

GWENNY: I'm not lying, you know I've been sick, it's morning sickness, happens when you're pregnant.

[Sid laughs.]

What are you laughing at?

SID: You, huh, it's a joke, innit?

GWENNY: I'm not, Jack, it's true.

SID: You're drunk, you need a bath.

GWENNY: No, I want to talk to you, about the baby.

SID: You're not having one.

GWENNY: I am, I am, why don't you believe me, I love you, Jack, I wouldn't lie to you.

[Sid looks at her, slowly realising what she's saying.]

SID: Hey come on, don't play games.

GWENNY: Jack?

SID: Do you know what you're saying? Do you?

GWENNY: Give me a hug, Jack, you're supposed to kiss me and tell me I'm the best woman in the world. Tell me you're happy, please tell me you're happy.

SID: Oh, fucking hell... get away from me....

[Gwenny tries to hug him but he pushes her away.]

GWENNY: Jack, I love you, we've made a baby, say you're happy.

SID: You're not having one.

[Silence.]

GWENNY: Do you want a drink?

[Passes him a bottle, but he throws it away.]

Do you want to go to bed and play then? Why don't you smile?

SID: Because you're my sister, you understand me?

GWENNY: No, you're not.

SID: I am, I am, game's over, Gwenny.

GWENNY: Gwenny? Who's Gwenny?

SID: Listen to me.

[Pause.]

Remember the books, I read and you read, about Jack Kerouac and Joyce Johnson.

GWENNY: A love story.

SID: Yeah, a love story. We liked it, remember, and remember things were going wrong, like when I didn't get the job on the Open Cast, and mam was ill?

GWENNY: The dinosaurs, we ran away from them.

SID: Yeah, and ever since we were small, mam told us that dad was in America, and you were writing letters to him, and we thought he'd ask us to go out and see him?

GWENNY: No.

SID: Say you do, you do. I said I was Jack, and you were Joyce.

GWENNY: No, but I know you're Jack and I'm Joyce.

SID: No, it was a game, a game you hear me? It was a game, we were upset, we believed it for a bit, but in the back of our minds we knew we were only playing, didn't we?

GWENNY: No Jack, I'm not playing — game, what game?

[Sid is exasperated.]

SID: Your name is Gwen, Gwenny Lewis.

[Silence.]

And I'm your brother, Sid Lewis, and your other brother isn't here, but we call him Boyo, don't we?

[Gwenny shakes her head and stares at him.]

GWENNY: Your name is Jack Kerouac, and you'll be with me forever. Why are you trying to confuse me?

SID: Let's talk about the baby, is it true you're going to have a baby?

GWENNY: Of course it's true, I wouldn't lie, I love you.

SID: Oh Jesus.

GWENNY: You don't love me, do you?

SID: I love you, Gwenny, but you're my sister, can't you see that?

GWENNY: Stop playing this game with me, I don't like it,

you're being odd, I don't like it.

[*Sid puts his arms around her.*]

SID: It's all lies, Gwenny, it's dreamland.

GWENNY: There's nothing wrong with that, I knew you'd take me there.

SID: What can I do, what can I do?

GWENNY: Just say you love me, Jack.

SID: Don't call me Jack, I'm not Jack, I never was Jack, and I'm not Jack now.

GWENNY: But I'm going to have your baby.

SID: It's fucking dream city, can't you see that?

GWENNY: Don't be ugly.

SID: I'm being ugly, because it is fucking ugly.

GWENNY: Don't swear.

SID: We've got to get rid of it, you've got to see a doctor.

GWENNY: No, no doctors.

SID: He can help us.

GWENNY: No doctors, they'll kill my baby.

SID: It's the only way.

GWENNY: No, get away from me, what's happened to you, Jack?

SID: It's wrong, Gwenny, I....

[*Grabbing her.*]

GWENNY: Get off me you're hurting the baby.

SID: We've got to get rid of it, Gwenny.

[*Gwenny hits him hard across the face. Sid pushes her away.*]

It's not all my fault, it's your fault too, but we've had it now, you hear me, we've had it.

GWENNY: You're a fraud.

SID: It's all dreamland, where's the... where's Boyo, got to find Boyo. Don't go out of the house you hear me, till I come back. He'll get a doctor, he'll help me, he's my brother, no babies, no way.

[Gwenny scorns him as drums and crashing cymbals play.]

GWENNY: You're a fucking fraud.

[Lights change. Boyo stands alone among some ruins. Sid approaches behind him. During the scene, Boyo can hardly look at his brother.]

SID: Boyo.

[Boyo turns round, looks at him.]

BOYO: Sid. *[flatly]*

SID: Yeah, it's me.

[Pause.]

BOYO: How's Gwenny?

SID: She's still in the house.

[Pause.]

BOYO: She told me she was pregnant, Sid.

SID: She's lying.

BOYO: She said it was yours.

SID: I told you it's lies.

BOYO: You haven't touched her, have you?

SID: No, she's in the house.

BOYO: Look at me, you bastard.

[Boyo grabs him.]

SID: It's all finished.

[Pause. Boyo releases him.]

You've got to help me, Boyo, you've got to help me. Gwenny says she's pregnant, she says it's me. What the fuck can I do, you've got to help me, Boyo?

BOYO: Get off me, get off, it's too late for that, Sid, too late, it's all fucked, all of it.

SID: You're not listening to me, she says she's pregnant, she's got to see a doctor, but she won't. I thought it was a game, Boyo, a game, but I didn't know. Gwenny, she can't see it, she thinks she's Joyce.

BOYO: Are you trying to tell me you were playing, that all the mad things that have been going on for the last few months was playing, what the fuck you take me for, uh?

SID: It's the truth, it was the shock, the old man, and then mam. And I was pissed all the time, I didn't know what I was doing.

[Boyo grabs him.]

BOYO: I'll tell you what you did, you slept with your own sister, you got me? You told me lie after lie, you bastard, and now you turn round to me and say, you didn't know what was going on? All the fuck-ing dreaming, and the yankage, and you say you were playing? Get off me.

SID: It's the truth, I didn't know who I was. I did think I was Jack for a bit, felt good. I'm fucking finished, that's why, you hear me. I'm on the scrap heap, I'm nearly thirty, Boyo, and the only job I've ever had is fucking gravedigging. I've had it.

[Pause.]

Jack had all the answers, we were on the same wavelength... but I didn't think it would turn out like this, and I don't know if she is pregnant, she won't see a doctor, Boyo, and she's killing herself — pills. You've got to help me, she doesn't know it was a game.

BOYO: Can't you see what you've done to us you sick bastard?

[Pushes him away.]

SID: We messed about a bit, Boyo, that's all, I don't....

BOYO: That's all? She doesn't know who she is, or you.

SID: It was the way she was dressing, all the suspenders, she was driving me mad, she was Joyce, but I didn't, Boyo, we never made it, we were always drinking. I've tried to tell her I'm Sid but she won't believe me... she still thinks she's in America or somewhere, she's not joking, Boyo. Why doesn't she stop and say she's Gwenny, why Boyo, why? Help me, Boyo, I'm your brother.

BOYO: Not any more you're not.

[Boyo kicks Sid in the groin, punches him. Sid hardly puts a hand out to stop him. To the music of Lou Reed's 'Perfect Day', Boyo strangles his brother. Sid dies. Boyo drags him off, weeping.]

[Lights up on Gwenny, walking round the room unsteadily with a bottle of tablets still in her hands.]

GWENNY: And he said in Iowa I know by now the children must be crying in the land where they let the children cry, and tonight the stars will be out... and God is Pooh Bear.

[She laughs then stops suddenly.]

Why did he say the children cry?

[Pause.]

Jack was a fraud, but I'll have a baby that will laugh and laugh forever.

98

[Pause.]

No I won't, he's gone to get a doctor, he wants to kill the baby, I won't let him come too far now, oops.

[Pause.]

He's left me on my own.

[Silence.]

I used to cry when I was younger.

[Gwenny pops a load of pills.]

The truth of it is he said he was a poet.

[Silence.]

I was born in a crowd now I'll die on my own.

[She falls over.]

Take the chains off your feet, brother... kiss me... kiss me. Got to get out of here fast, baby, I've got the Benzedrine, nice sweets. Too many sweets, I'm sick. *[she vomits]* Where's my dad and mam, make me better... gone, all without me, always run away... no home, no... I'm all right, Jack.

[She drinks again and takes more pills, and vomits.]

We can go out in the moonlight when the dinosaurs are sleeping. They've eaten the dragon, and found my father... tin men... clankety clank... boom buddy boom... buddy hiccup clanks... the wind will make them feel better.

[Silence.]

I won't have a donkey will I? Trecco bay donkey as a little boy?

[She tries to get up.]

Oh... my feet are like lead, look... all pins and needles... won't be long now... I can't get up... and now's my chance when the world's asleep, but my legs won't walk, won't run, look at them, all those thousands of miles down my leg... the plains of Iowa, the girl from the prairie got a ladder in her stocking, stairway to Heaven, my belly will grow like a new mountain, it will have climbers on it, I'm conquered forever... all creepy with hard hands and fingers... get off me... get him off me... GET HIM OFF ME...

[Silence.]

All quiet in a forgotten town... music I need... I'll have to lie on the bed... but Jack will be there and he'll want to breed with me....

[Boyo enters in darkness.]

BOYO: Gwenny?

GWENNY: Here he comes, the breeder, who doesn't want to know. I'm keeping my baby, go away, if you've come to kill it.

BOYO: Gwenny?

GWENNY: I can't feel my arms. Please mister, can you tell me... why I can't... move? You want my breast, Jack, suck if you like but save some for the baby....

BOYO: Help me, Gwenny.

GWENNY: It's... it's... raining.

[Pause.]

I... think I'm going to... all lost... my way... you know... Sssleep....

BOYO: Gwenny!

[Lights fade slowly to blackout.]

THE END

Flowers Of The Dead Red Sea

Notes to the Original Production

Flowers Of The Dead Red Sea was first performed in the Theatres and Nations Festival at Tramway, Glasgow on 9 September, 1991. The play has since been revised and of the original cast, only two parts remain.

Cast

Mock............................Richard Lynch
Joe................................Russell Gomer

Music........................Gareth Whittock
Set and Lighting....................Ian Hill
Directed by............. Edward Thomas

Special thanks to cast members Wyndham Price, Eddie Ladd, Mark Knight and Lesley Rooney.

Start

[*A world of chains, knives, steel, blood and falling objects. Mock and Joe are half-naked, bloody and vulnerable in a dangerous world.*]

[*Darkness. An alarm bell sounds. Mock and Joe rise and prepare for work in early dawn light, sharpening knives, hoisting carcasses. Joe wears a crash helmet. Tom Jones' 'It's Not Unusual' may play. Joe counts.*]

JOE: 10, 11, 12, 13, 14, 15, 16, 17, 18, 19, 20, 21, 22, 23, 24, 25.

MOCK: Are you sure?

JOE: I counted them twice.

MOCK: Count again.

JOE: There is no need to count again.

MOCK: It is important to me, Joe.

JOE: If you don't believe me, count them yourself.

MOCK: I don't want to count them myself.

JOE: Then you'll just have to believe me.

MOCK: I can't.

JOE: Why not?

MOCK: You're a difficult man to believe.

JOE: No more than anyone else.

MOCK: That's not the point.

JOE: Then what is the point?

MOCK: The dicky bow.

JOE: What about it?

MOCK: It never came from Tom Jones.

JOE: It did.

MOCK: It never.

JOE: Bollocks.

MOCK: Truth.

JOE: He once sang a song in it.

MOCK: What song?

JOE: 'Delilah'.

MOCK: Crap.

JOE: 'It's Not Unusual'.

MOCK: Crap again.

JOE: 'I'm Coming Home'.

MOCK: Crap, crap, crap.

JOE: It's not crap.

MOCK: That dicky bow is not Tom Jones's.

JOE: He threw it to the crowd.

MOCK: Were you part of the crowd?

JOE: No, but I bought it from someone who was.

MOCK: You've changed your story.

JOE: It cost twenty quid.

MOCK: Last time you said he gave it to you for nothing.

JOE: I never said that.

MOCK: "Joe," you said, said Tom, "this is my dicky bow, have it."

JOE: I never said that.

MOCK: Neither did Tom.

JOE: He said it to someone else.

MOCK: Not you?

JOE: Not me.

MOCK: Then who?

JOE: The woman I bought it off.

MOCK: What was her name?

JOE: I forget.

MOCK: Where did she get it?

JOE: She said Las Vegas.

MOCK: And you believe her?

JOE: SHE WAS A BIG FAN!

MOCK: You bought a dicky from....

JOE: Not any dicky.

MOCK: What then?

JOE: This dicky.

MOCK: Jesus.

JOE: This dicky is the dicky in question, Mock. Not any fucking dicky.

MOCK: Tom or Harry.

JOE: What?

MOCK: Tom or Harry.

JOE: Was that a joke, Mock?

MOCK: It was.

JOE: A laugh?

MOCK: Yes.

JOE: You were laughing at me.

MOCK: I was.

JOE: You bastard.

MOCK: You had it coming.

JOE: You shit.

MOCK: I am no shit.

JOE: You need me and yet you laugh at me.

MOCK: You do the same to me.

JOE: I'm all you've got.

MOCK: You salt the skins.

JOE: I wash the floor.

MOCK: You pull the chains.

JOE: I put the brains and guts in bins and you laugh?

MOCK: It was only a joke.

JOE: I'm not laughing.

MOCK: Tom and Harry are friends of Dicky but Dicky's a bow.

JOE: Not any bow, Tom's bow.

MOCK: Bollocks.

JOE: True, I bought it from a big fan who saw him in New York.

MOCK: When?

JOE: A while back.

MOCK: Where?

JOE: In a queue.

MOCK: A queue?

JOE: To one of his concerts.

MOCK: Don't tell me lies.

JOE: You are impossible.

MOCK: Your story has changed.

JOE: Fuck the story, feel the velvet.

MOCK: No.

JOE: Why not?

MOCK: I hate velvet.

JOE: You hate Tom.

MOCK: I like Tom.

JOE: You don't hum his songs.

MOCK: His songs are not for humming.

JOE: I hum.

MOCK: You stink.

JOE: So do you.

MOCK: I'm a killer.

JOE: I'm a salter of skins.

MOCK: This is a slaughter-house.

JOE: It hums to high heaven.

MOCK: Not to Tom's songs.

JOE: No.

MOCK: With the stench of death.

JOE: If only you sang.

MOCK: I can't sing.

JOE: It would hide the stench.

MOCK: I have no voice.

JOE: A fucking whistle would do.

MOCK: I'm tone deaf and too busy.

JOE: Hum, Mock.

MOCK: I don't want to hum.

JOE: Sing, Mock.

MOCK: I don't want to sing.

JOE: Fucking whistle then.

MOCK: THIS IS NO TIME FOR WHISTLING.

JOE: JESUS, THIS IS IMPOSSIBLE.

MOCK: Don't you think I know that?

JOE: I don't know what you know.

MOCK: I know what I know.

JOE: What do you know?

MOCK: I won't kill any more than my daily capacity.

JOE: Daily capacity?

MOCK: Forty a day.

JOE: Don't talk crap.

MOCK: It's not crap.

JOE: The job won't be finished.

MOCK: We'll have to turn them away.

JOE: You can't turn them away when they've come here to be slaughtered.

MOCK: Then they will just have to revolt!

JOE: Revolt?

MOCK: Revolt, yes revolt.

JOE: There is not a bone of revolt in their bodies.

MOCK: What do you know?

JOE: I have held the beast's heads and watched you shoot them dead. I have seen you put knives in the throats of lambs; watched you shave the hair off pigs in a boiling tub, feed nails and skin and flesh to dogs and still it is all silence, meek submission. They would rather starve in a crowded pen than revolt.

MOCK: There will be no other solution.

JOE: Won't there, Mock?

MOCK: No, this steel was given to me by my father to put an edge on a blade to kill forty a day. FORTY AND NO MORE. If forty come in here, meet with my knife, leave their better parts on hooks and their head, feet and skins on the floor, I will know that I'll have killed them with dignity, with a sharp blade; if I kill any more my blade will be blunt and they will die in shame. I am a craftsman, Joe, and I will not work in a bloodbath of shame.

JOE: Jesus, Mock.

MOCK: Jesus Mock or not, that will be it for the day. You'll have to sit down, relax and put up your feet.

JOE: Will I, Mock, will I?

MOCK: There will be no other solution, Joe.

JOE: No?

MOCK: No.

[Pause.]

JOE: We'll just see what Cragg has to say about that.

MOCK: Cragg is a bastard.

JOE: Cragg owns this killing house.

MOCK: I am not afraid of Cragg.

JOE: He will be angry, Mock, and he is a powerful man.

MOCK: FUCK HIS POWER AND ANGER, I HAD A DREAM.

JOE: A dream?

MOCK: I dreamt last night I was a bucket.

JOE: A what?

MOCK: A bucket.

JOE: What kind of bucket?

MOCK: A steel bucket.

JOE: Yeah?

MOCK: Yeah.

JOE: What about it?

MOCK: I was being filled with water, I couldn't breathe.

JOE: You were drowning?

MOCK: I was drowning.

JOE: Jesus.

MOCK: I started to panic, I tried to cry for help, but the water kept filling my lungs, I couldn't shout, there was a skylight above me, and above the skylight were the stars.

JOE: The stars?

MOCK: The moon and the stars laughing.

JOE: The hanging moon and the stars.

MOCK: This was *my* dream, Joe.

JOE: I was helping out.

MOCK: I don't need help.

JOE: I was....

MOCK: You were nowhere in sight, you never featured.

JOE: So?

MOCK: It was only me and the stars and the water.

JOE: You were a bucket.

MOCK: I was a bucket looking up at the stars.

JOE: A steel bucket.

MOCK: A silver steel bucket drowning in water.

JOE: What did you do?

MOCK: I started to rock, from one side to the other. I made waves in the water, Joe, by rocking back and fore. I rocked and I rocked till the water started to spill over the top and still I was rocking, till crrraaaaa-sssssh.

JOE: You woke up?

MOCK: No.

JOE: What then?

MOCK: I tipped over and landed on my side, steel bucket against stone floor and the water streamed every-where and ended up in the gutter. Then I heard shouting. There was a man.

JOE: What man?

MOCK: Cragg. He was angry, Joe, big red face on him, shouting and screaming that I was a problem bucket. He was a bastard, Joe.

JOE: Cragg is a bastard.

MOCK: I was still getting my breath back when he ran towards me and shunt, he kicked me hard in the side and I went rolling like a top right into the wall, feeling numb.

JOE: That bastard.

MOCK: He kicked me, Joe! I was only trying to breathe!

JOE: You were a drowning bucket.

MOCK: He kicked the bucket, Joe!

JOE: What?

MOCK: He kicked the fucking bucket, he died.

JOE: Jesus.

MOCK: When I came round he was flat out on the floor as dead as dead, but I was still here.

[Mock starts to laugh loudly, enjoying the joke. Joe does not find it so funny.]

I AM STILL HERE!

JOE: Was that a joke, Mock?

MOCK: No joke, it was a dream.

JOE: You made it up.

MOCK: No way.

JOE: You lied.

MOCK: All true.

JOE: I don't believe you, Mock.

MOCK: I know what I dreamt, it was my dream!

JOE: Sod your dream.

MOCK: You're only jealous.

JOE: I am not jealous.

MOCK: Because you never featured, you weren't in it, you were invisible.

JOE: I don't fucking care, Mock, I can dream for myself.

MOCK: You don't dream.

JOE: How do you know?

MOCK: You told me.

JOE: I never.

MOCK: You fucking did.

JOE: When?

MOCK: Not long ago.

JOE: I'm a light sleeper.

MOCK: You were asleep when I woke last night.

JOE: When did you wake?

MOCK: After my dream, I heard the antics of rats.

JOE: Where was I?

MOCK: Asleep over there.

JOE: I must have dozed off.

MOCK: That's where I heard the antics of rats.

JOE: What antics?

MOCK: Squeaking and scratching not far from your head.

JOE: The bastards, did you throw something at them?

MOCK: I didn't want to wake you.

JOE: I would have awakened.

MOCK: There were three of them, a parent and two nippers, squeaking.

JOE: Jesus Christ, Mock, you know how I fear rats!

MOCK: Dirty bastards.

JOE: What happened next?

MOCK: They saw me shuffle and ran away.

JOE: You should have thrown the bucket at them.

MOCK: I did.

JOE: Impossible, I would have woken up in the racket.

MOCK: You stayed asleep, Joe.

JOE: I'm a light sleeper.

MOCK: You never stirred.

JOE: I WOULD NEVER HAVE SLEPT THROUGH THE NOISE OF A CRASHING BUCKET!

MOCK: You did.

JOE: Impossible.

MOCK: You snored through the commotion, dead to the world. You were in the land of the dead, Joe.

JOE: I AM NOT DEAD.

MOCK: How do you know?

JOE: My nails are still growing.

[Mock takes Joe's hands and looks.]

MOCK: Bitten to the bone.

JOE: My toe nails.

MOCK: Covered in sock and boot.

JOE: Sock and boot for protection.

MOCK: Take off your boots.

JOE: Why should I?

MOCK: To prove you are living.

JOE: I know I am living.

MOCK: That is not good enough.

JOE: What is it you want from me, Mock?

MOCK: The truth.

JOE: The truth does not lie in my boot.

MOCK: It lies in your toe nails.

JOE: My nails are still growing.

MOCK: Then prove it.

JOE: Why should I prove it?

MOCK: To show me that you're here.

JOE: You know that I'm here.

MOCK: You might be asleep.

JOE: I MIGHT BE ASLEEP, BUT AT LEAST I DON'T SLEEPWALK.

MOCK: I don't sleepwalk.

JOE: I have seen you.

MOCK: When?

JOE: A few nights ago. I threw two buckets of water over you, but you never woke up.

MOCK: You bastard.

JOE: I put a chain around your ankle.

MOCK: You chained me?

JOE: For your own protection, Mock!

MOCK: You know how I hate being chained.

JOE: You were damaging yourself!

MOCK: How do you know?

JOE: You got up from the floor, howled like a wolf, stood on one leg like this, and ran headlong into the wall head first shouting "shame, shame".

MOCK: I never.

JOE: I saw you.

MOCK: I don't believe you.

JOE: I thought you were dead.

MOCK: Straight up?

JOE: Truth.

MOCK: There's no lump.

JOE: There was yesterday.

MOCK: How do you know?

JOE: I noticed.

MOCK: You could have said.

JOE: It would have upset you.

MOCK: I am not fragile.

JOE: You are, Mock.

MOCK: Jesus.

JOE: Last night was even worse.

MOCK: You were asleep.

JOE: I was pretending.

MOCK: Bollocks.

JOE: Not bollocks, you said you were drowning.

MOCK: I never.

JOE: Down on the beach, your head in the sand and your feet in the sea, you said you were tired.

MOCK: I never went anywhere.

JOE: "WHAT'S HAPPENED TO MEMORY?" YOU SHOUTED.

MOCK: I did?

JOE: I heard you, last night, in your sleep you were afraid.

MOCK: That's no crime.

JOE: "HAVE I DROWNED?" YOU SHOUTED, "AM I DEAD?" YOU SCREAMED.

MOCK: No.

JOE: Yes, Mock, yes, "Break the silence," you said, and with that you sunk your teeth into your arm violently, like I've seen you finish off fried chicken legs in a hurry. You'd have a nasty scar there if I hadn't stopped you.

MOCK: You didn't stop me.

JOE: Then look at your arm, Mock!

MOCK: Why should I?

JOE: It's my proof.

[Mock looks at his arm.]

MOCK: Teeth marks.

JOE: I was telling the truth.

MOCK: They may not be mine.

JOE: Are you accusing me?

MOCK: Might be.

JOE: Jesus!

MOCK: You might be trying to get at me.

JOE: I'm not trying to get at you, I'm trying to help you.

MOCK: How do I know that?

JOE: You've got to trust me.

MOCK: I don't trust a soul.

JOE: I did not bite your arm.

MOCK: Who did then? Rats?

JOE: You did it yourself!

MOCK: I never.

JOE: I KNOW WHAT I SAW.

[Suddenly a rusty and smashed pram falls from the sky with a crash.]

MOCK: JESUS!

[Pause.]

JOE: It's a pram.

MOCK: I CAN SEE IT'S A PRAM, BUT WHY DOES A

RUSTY OLD PRAM FALL DOWN FROM OUR SKIES?

JOE: There are many phenomena in this world that are beyond us, Mock.

MOCK: This falling is beyond comprehension.

JOE: You must not take it to heart, Mock.

MOCK: How can I not take it to heart when it threatens the core of my sanity?

JOE: It's a problem.

MOCK: IT'S A FUCKING CRISIS.

[Mock starts to smash the pram violently as Joe laughs, watching him. Lights change as Joe hoists up another corpse on chains, leaving it bleeding into a bucket. Music fades, Mock moves away from the pram, exhausted. Joe counts.]

JOE: 26, 27, 28, 29, 30.

MOCK: Are you sure?

JOE: I counted them twice.

[Mock looks away, disgusted.]

JOE: Do you know what I think?

MOCK: No, I've got no idea.

JOE: We are like two men in a boat.

MOCK: What two men in a boat?

JOE: Any two men in a boat.

MOCK: I am not in a boat.

JOE: One man turns to the other and says "I feel sick," the other nods, turns round and says "I don't."

MOCK: I feel sick.

JOE: Exactly, and I am the one who is not.

MOCK: I don't care who you are.

JOE: You don't fucking know who I am.

MOCK: I do.

JOE: Then speak.

MOCK: Your name is Joe, you salt the skins, you wash the floor, you put the feet and guts in bins.

JOE: How long have I worked here?

MOCK: A few months.

JOE: Bollocks!

MOCK: A few years.

JOE: "A few years," he says, "a few years." After all the toil I've put in here he says, "a few years." You can't even remember when you first fucking met me.

MOCK: So what, can you?

JOE: That's beside the point.

MOCK: Exactly.

JOE: You should be ashamed of yourself.

MOCK: The only shame I have is that I gave you the job.

JOE: You had to give me the job.

MOCK: I didn't.

JOE: You did, the boiling breath of commerce was blow-ing too fiercely down the back of your neck.

MOCK: I was a craftsman who needed some help.

JOE: You wanted a skivvy.

MOCK: I wanted someone with dignity, self-respect.

JOE: Fuck self-respect, fuck dignity.

MOCK: Exactly.

JOE: What you mean?

MOCK: You look ridiculous.

JOE: I no longer fear ridicule, the world has taken me beyond any fear of the ridiculous.

MOCK: You should do.

JOE: I haven't a choice.

MOCK: You could take off your crash helmet.

JOE: I will not take off my crash helmet, Mock, these are dangerous times, things falling apart at the seams.

MOCK: Things are not falling apart.

JOE: Of course they are, falling about our ears, this entire slaughter-house has been furnished by things that have fallen about us, cooker, washing machine, frozen chicken, hair drier, microwave.

MOCK: Microwave?

JOE: Yes, microwave.

MOCK: I don't remember a microwave.

JOE: It fell a few days ago.

MOCK: I never saw it.

JOE: I showed it to you, I said, "What do you think about this then?"

MOCK: You didn't say that about any microwave.

JOE: I did, I'm sure I did.

MOCK: No, you've got it wrong there you said that to me when the chair came.

JOE: What chair?

MOCK: That chair.

JOE: I never.

MOCK: You did.

JOE: Did I?

MOCK: I can see it now, you held out the chair to me and said, "What do you think about this then?"

JOE: Jesus.

MOCK: And I said great and took it off you.

JOE: Then what?

MOCK: Than I sat down on it.

JOE: What did I do?

MOCK: You stood.

JOE: Why?

MOCK: Because, Joe, there is only one chair.

JOE: And you sat on it.

MOCK: Yes.

JOE: Typical, that is bloody typical, I drew your attention to a chair that you'd never before set your eyes on, you say "great," take it off me and park your arse on it, leaving me standing here like a lemon in a crash helmet.

MOCK: And whose responsibility is that?

JOE: What?

MOCK: The crash helmet.

JOE: Mine.

MOCK: Exactly. So don't blame me that you stand to be ridiculed.

JOE: THIS CRASH HELMET PROVIDES ME WITH MY ONLY PROTECTION FROM THE RAVAGES OF PROGRESS AND THE GENERAL GOOD.

MOCK: We are not progressing.

JOE: No, we're fucked.

MOCK: And I hate the General Good.

JOE: So do I, but this helmet will protect me.

MOCK: It won't.

JOE: It will.

MOCK: Bollocks, it was General Good who slaughtered red Indians, wiped them off the face of the earth and murdered the buffaloes, turning the prairies into blood and that helmet won't stop him from smashing your head either.

JOE: MY HELMET WILL NOT BE SMASHED.

MOCK: COURSE IT WILL, HE'S PROBABLY WAITING TO CRUSH IT ALREADY, CRUSH YOUR HEAD WITH THE HOOVES OF HIS HORSE, his shiny white horse, whinny, whinny, white and strong, his muscles are taut, his flanks stained with sweat, he chews on his bridle, Joe, this horse must go, THE STRONG WHITE HORSE OF GENERAL GOOD, THE ANGRY STALLION OF PROGRESS, HE WILL NOT BE DENIED, JOE.

          [Mock does the noise of a horse and whips off Joe's helmet.]

JOE: GIVE ME MY HELMET BACK, YOU BASTARD.

MOCK: The horse is away, Joe, and Mr Good is on its back sucking a mint, the fresh breath of Mr Good, Joe, can you smell it?

JOE: I WANT MY HELMET.

MOCK: You'll have to chase after him for it, Joe, run like fuck as the bugle sounds.

          [Mock does the sound of a bugle.]

JOE: Don't do this to me, Mock, I....

MOCK: Run like fuck after Mr Good, to pastures lush and green, cool mountain springs, till he turns the land to weed and dust and drinks the springs to stone and pebble and then you arrive, Joe, thirsty and exhausted but the bugle sounds, Joe, and he's off again but you can't go back, you can't go on, you don't know what to do, all you can do is ask for your helmet.

JOE: GIVE ME MY FUCKING HELMET.

[Mock pulls Joe up close.]

MOCK: You'll find your helmet on the parched and yellow earth, Joe, it'll be dusty from the long journey, but you'll pick it up because it is your helmet, you'll smile and look inside it then your face will turn to stone, because inside it will be the crushed good half of your brain.

JOE: STOP THIS FUCKING RHETORIC, MOCK, IT IS INSULTING MY EARS.

MOCK: RHETORIC?

JOE: Rhetoric, hot air, bombast, ornamentation, sheer contrivance.

MOCK: I was speaking from my heart, Joe.

JOE: Your heart is good, but it is no fucking poet.

MOCK: I was searching for definition.

JOE: Things can no longer be defined, now give me my helmet back.

MOCK: It won't protect you, Joe.

JOE: I know it won't protect me.

MOCK: Then why do you wear it?

JOE: To protect the bit of my brain that still remains.

MOCK: What bit is that?

JOE: The bad bit.

MOCK: What about the good bit?

JOE: That is already crushed, like my mother's and my father's, my grandparents and theirs. I am the progeny of crushed good brain, the history of crushed good brain, I am the future of a million crushed good brains, now give me back my helmet before the rest gets crushed for good.

        [Joe holds out his arm for the helmet. Mock hands it back to him.]

JOE: Thanks.

        [Pause.]

MOCK: I am still good, Joe.

JOE: Good? You?

MOCK: Yes.

JOE: Bollocks.

MOCK: I am.

JOE: You're sick.

MOCK: I'm not.

JOE: You just said you were.

MOCK: When?

JOE: When you were the man in the boat.

MOCK: I am not talking of boats.

JOE: You were a minute ago.

MOCK: What is a minute to a good man born with high hopes?

JOE: High hopes?

MOCK: Yes.

JOE: You?

MOCK: Yes.

JOE: Don't make me laugh.

MOCK: It is no joke.

JOE: Hopes to do what?

MOCK: Something, somewhere, someone.

JOE: Like what?

MOCK: I don't know.

JOE: Like what?

MOCK: A boxer.

JOE: Fuck off.

MOCK: I did.

JOE: You'd be shit.

MOCK: How do you know?

JOE: You've got a glass jaw.

MOCK: I'm a southpaw.

JOE: Southpaw, southpaw.

MOCK: I lead with my right.

JOE: Show.

MOCK: I'll show.

[Mock sets up as a boxer.]

MOCK: There.

JOE: Is that it?

MOCK: I'm out of training.

JOE: Training would never help you.

MOCK: How do you know?

JOE: Move.

MOCK: What?

JOE: Move, let me see how you move.

MOCK: There's no-one to move to.

JOE: Pretend.

MOCK: Imagine?

JOE: Exactly.

MOCK: It's not easy.

JOE: To imagine?

MOCK: To box.

JOE: To shadow box.

MOCK: Now?

JOE: Now.

[Pause. Mock contemplates it.]

MOCK: I can't.

JOE: I'm waiting.

MOCK: I FUCKING CAN'T MOVE.

JOE: You said you were a boxer.

MOCK: ONLY IF THINGS WERE DIFFERENT.

JOE: You've got no grit.

MOCK: I HAVE.

JOE: Then box.

MOCK: I can't.

JOE: Why not?

MOCK: I DON'T KNOW.

JOE: I do.

MOCK: WHY?

JOE: Because you are not good.

MOCK: I AM STILL GOOD.

JOE: NO.

MOCK: YES.

JOE: NO.

MOCK: YES, FUCKING YES, FUCKING YES, YES, YES.

[Mock is upset. Pause.]

JOE: You are no longer happy, Mock.

MOCK: I am.

JOE: You're not, Mock.

MOCK: Is this not a smile?

[Trying to smile.]

JOE: It's a nothing smile.

MOCK: What about this one?

JOE: No better.

MOCK: This is.

JOE: That's not a smile, it's a rattle.

MOCK: I am not rattling.

JOE: You are rattling with fear, Mock.

MOCK: I am not afraid.

JOE: You have a problem.

MOCK: I do not have a problem.

JOE: In there the problem is, Mock, inside your head, your precious head, your floating brain. There is a cat in there, Mock, lurking, a fat alley cat, licking its paws, cleaning its whiskers, sitting on a dustbin, sunning itself on your grey mass of tissue. He has had a feast, Mock, a big feast. He's eaten a fish, a fresh fish, a nice fresh fish, your fresh fish, Mock, your fresh fish of happiness.

MOCK: No.

JOE: Yes.

MOCK: I am happy.

JOE: You are not happy.

MOCK: Yes.

JOE: No.

MOCK: I have my fishy and there is no cat.

JOE: Nibble, nibble, slurp, slurp, hiccup, hiccup, happy cat eated fishy, left only bones in Mocky's head, no fun Mocky, no happy Mocky, fallen Mocky, sad Mocky, rattling Mocky, rattling bones.

MOCK: I am not rattling.

JOE: I rattle, you rattle, the whole fucking world rattles.

MOCK: I am not fucking rattling, Joe.

JOE: "Dem bones, dem bones, dem dry bones, etc...."

MOCK: Stop singing, Joe.

JOE: "Dem bones, dem bones, dem dryyy bones, etc..."

MOCK: This is no time for singing, Joe.

JOE: "Dem bones, dem bones, all in the name of the Lord."

[Mock threatens Joe with a knife.]

MOCK: STOP FUCKING SINGING, JOE.

[Silence. Joe looks at the knife.]

JOE: Put the knife down, Mock.

MOCK: It's my knife.

JOE: It is now, but it was me who bought it for you.

MOCK: Don't talk crap.

JOE: I'm not talking crap.

MOCK: When?

JOE: A while ago.

MOCK: From where?

JOE: Saudi.

MOCK: Saudi?

JOE: Saudi Arabia.

MOCK: Jesus.

JOE: I bought you that knife from a bedouin in the desert.

MOCK: A bedouin?

JOE: He was riding a camel.

MOCK: It must have been hot.

JOE: He didn't wear trousers.

MOCK: What was he wearing?

JOE: He was wearing a sheet.

MOCK: A bed sheet?

JOE: Looked like it.

MOCK: In the desert?

JOE: It kept him cool.

MOCK: What did he sleep on?

JOE: I never asked.

MOCK: Did you ride on his camel?

JOE: He never offered.

MOCK: You were in trousers?

JOE: It's the hottest I've been.

MOCK: You should have known better.

JOE: I never prepared.

MOCK: You were in a desert, Joe.

JOE: I lost my way.

MOCK: You could have died.

JOE: I was dying of thirst.

MOCK: He saved your life.

JOE: I'll be eternally grateful.

MOCK: What was he doing?

JOE: Travelling around.

MOCK: Touting for business.

JOE: He sold me this knife, I bought it for you.

MOCK: Me!

JOE: You, it was a present.

MOCK: I forgot.

JOE: Forget it.

MOCK: I appreciate it.

JOE: Good.

MOCK: It's a good knife.

JOE: Yes.

MOCK: BUT IT WON'T KILL MORE THAN FORTY A DAY.

JOE: We'll see what Cragg has to say about that, shall we?

MOCK: Fuck Cragg, this was a craft taught me by my father, he was a good teacher, Joe.

JOE: He threw a good arrow too.

MOCK: You knew my father?

JOE: I watched him play darts in a pub.

MOCK: What pub?

JOE: The Old Drum and Monkey, he was the star of the show, he drank seven pints of lager and still threw a straight dart.

MOCK: He kept a steady hand?

JOE: Straight as an arrow. I saw him in a final.

MOCK: What final?

JOE: In the first set he threw two nine dart finishes.

MOCK: Straight up.

JOE: Straight up, with the first six darts he threw a hundred and eighty twice.

MOCK: That gave him three-sixty.

JOE: Correct.

MOCK: Then what?

JOE: With his first dart he threw treble twenty.

MOCK: Brings him up to four-twenty with eighty-one left.

JOE: CORRECT, CORRECT!

MOCK: THEN TELL ME THE FINISH, TELL ME THE FUCKING FINISH.

JOE: His second was a corker.

MOCK: Treble nineteen?

JOE: On the button.

MOCK: YEEEES, A DOUBLE TWELVE TO FINISH.

JOE: THEN CAME THE FINISH.

MOCK: Tell me, tell me.

[Pause.]

JOE: He took a drag of his smoke.

MOCK: Embassy No. 1's.

JOE: Correct.

MOCK: Next?

JOE: He took a sip of his pint.

MOCK: Tennent's Extra.

JOE: Correct. Drunk three-quarters way down.

MOCK: Next?

JOE: He took his position, nine feet from the board. He looked at the floor.

MOCK: Arranging himself.

JOE: THE BALANCE, MOCK. THE FRAGILE BALANCE.

MOCK: And? And?

JOE: With his head, still looking down at the floor, he raised his eyes to the board, he let them settle on his target.

MOCK: Double twelve.

JOE: Double twelve.

MOCK: Always a bastard.

JOE: Every time referee, every time.

MOCK: And?

JOE: He looked at the twelve like a hunter stalking a deer.

MOCK: A deer hunter.

JOE: A deer stalker! Then his eyes narrowed down the target, not a twelve, not a treble twelve, but a double twelve.

MOCK: DOUBLE TWELVE, DOUBLE TWELVE, GO FOR IT, DADDY, DADDY, GO, GO!

JOE: He lent on his front foot, lifted the dart, let his arm pull back till relaxed... then threw.

MOCK: THUD.

JOE: RIGHT IN THE HEART OF THE DOUBLE!

MOCK: YEEES.

JOE: YEEES.

[They celebrate wildly, then come to a stop.]

MOCK: Was he a star, Joe?

JOE: He was a star, Mock.

MOCK: Did the crowd shout?

JOE: The crowd shouted, Mock, they were ecstatic.

MOCK: Did he have them in the palm of his hand, Joe?

JOE: Like a lamb to a bottle, Mock.

MOCK: Was he happy, Joe?

JOE: He was happy, Mock. He was the happiest man I ever saw, you should be proud of him.

MOCK: I am, Joe, I am.

JOE: He's one of the few, Mock, a rare breed.

MOCK: I'm the son of my father.

JOE: You must miss him.

MOCK: I lost touch with him.

JOE: How do you mean?

MOCK: He wandered away.

JOE: You don't know where he is?

MOCK: No, do you?

JOE: Yes.

MOCK: Where is he?

JOE: He died, Mock.

MOCK: He what?

JOE: He's dead, Mock, I saw him fall.

MOCK: JESUS CHRIST. NOBODY TOLD ME!

JOE: I thought you knew, Mock.

MOCK: I did not know.

JOE: I would have told you, Mock, but....

MOCK: BUT... BUT... THE TYRANNY OF BUTS, MY FATHER IS DEAD, JOE.

[Mock starts to break down.]

JOE: I'm sorry, Mock.

MOCK: FUCK OFF WILL YOU, JUST FUCK OFF AND LET ME GRIEVE.

[Mock weeps as Joe watches. Daylight goes to darkness, music and lights fade to black. Mock and Joe sleep.]

MOCK: *[in darkness]* What's happened to memory, Joe? *[pause]* Joe? *[pause]* JOE!

[Silence. Darkness gives way to a dawn light. Fade in the sound of an incoming tide. Light is only on Mock.]

MOCK: I was in a town, but I could hear an incoming tide. I look around but don't recognise anyone and no-one recognises me. I'm afraid and I start to run, into a park where I see a child sitting on a swing, crying, he said he'd lost his brother.

[Pause.]

It could have been you, Joe.

[Pause.]

Joe?

[Joe doesn't respond.]

Horrible silence, horrible, hanging silence. Not a bird sings, not a leaf rustles, not a word is said, not a word is spoken. Everything floats by past my ears, past my lips, a million words passing, a whole language, a way of life, a people drowning, a mother, father, grandmother, grandfather, daughter, son, sister, brother passing by. Silent, sad, unmarked, peaceful, mad but sad, dead sad. I don't know who I am. Where am I?

[Pause.]

I look at a house. It is terraced, painted green. A small garden of wild flowers, a washing line, a bike sitting on its handlebars and saddle with its chain off. It looks like mine. I used to have a bike like that. We rode it in the summer, me and... my brother. Then I walk into the house... and I see her.

[Pause.]

She is an artist. She paints with oil on canvas. Sea horses and a heavy sky, a moon or sun of red. She is naked, but she dances on the sea, her long hair flows, her arms reach up, perhaps she is laughing, perhaps she is free. She is sprinkling yellow flowers on a dead red sea.

[Pause.]

She turns and looks at me, I feel I should know her... I think that I used to love her.... She said art can save culture.

[Pause.]

Joe? JOE!

[Sound of alarm bell and drums. Lights change, Joe springs into action and hoists a corpse on chains, lets it bleed into a bucket. Joe counts.]

JOE: 31, 32, 33, 34, 35.

MOCK: How was the funeral?

JOE: Very black, very wet, very windy.

MOCK: It rained?

JOE: It thundered.

MOCK: Many turn out?

JOE: It was packed.

MOCK: Where was he buried?

JOE: Next to your mother.

MOCK: She was an angel.

JOE: They were buried together.

MOCK: Was there beer and sandwiches?

JOE: Plenty, and crisps in bowls.

MOCK: Where was the spread?

JOE: In the Old Drum and Monkey.

MOCK: I should have been there.

JOE: Nobody told you.

MOCK: I wasn't to know.

JOE: It wasn't your fault, Mock.

MOCK: WHERE THE FUCK WAS MY BROTHER?

JOE: Your brother?

MOCK: I had a brother. Is it funny to have a brother, Joe?

JOE: It's the first time you've made any mention.

MOCK: It's the first time I've needed to.

JOE: Where is he?

MOCK: He decided to flower away from his roots.

JOE: Where did he go?

MOCK: I think he went East.

JOE: East?

MOCK: He was a sunshine boy who went in search of the sun.

JOE: What was his name?

MOCK: His name?

JOE: What was his name, Mock?

MOCK: He didn't have one.

JOE: Everyone has a name.

MOCK: That is no guarantee for remembrance.

JOE: You can't remember his name?

MOCK: I CAN'T FUCKING REMEMBER, I CAN'T FUCK-ING REMEMBER.

JOE: HE WAS YOUR BROTHER, MOCK.

MOCK: HE STOLE MY DICKY BOW.

JOE: You had a dicky bow?

MOCK: Did you think you were the only one?

JOE: I....

MOCK: All over the world, Joe, from Buenos Aires to Kathmandu, from Amsterdam to Nova Scotia, from Iceland to Zimbabwe, there is someone, somewhere stepping out in the street with a dicky bow around their neck.

[Takes Joe's dicky from around his neck.]

JOE: On a white shirt.

MOCK: On a white shirt, yes.

JOE: And cuff-links.

MOCK: Yes, yes, cuff-links.

JOE: And a stiff collar?

MOCK: Not necessarily.

JOE: And trousers.

MOCK: And trousers, yes.

JOE: You must never forget your trousers.

MOCK: No, a man doesn't know who he is without his trousers.

JOE: Exactly.

          [Mock checks to see if he's wearing trousers. He is and he smiles. Joe checks, he is also and he too smiles.]

JOE: Have you always worn trousers, Mock?

MOCK: For as long as I can remember.

JOE: What about when you're with a woman?

MOCK: With a woman?

JOE: A naked woman, lying on a silk sheet bed.

MOCK: I'd take off my trousers and fold them on the chair.

JOE: And if there wasn't a chair?

MOCK: I'd leave them on the floor.

JOE: Would you still know who you are?

MOCK: Course I would.

JOE: How?

MOCK: Because I'd remember how I'd felt before I took them off.

JOE: How did you feel?

MOCK: Strong, expectant, erect, watched.

JOE: Watched?

MOCK: I'd be watched by the woman.

JOE: Do you like being watched?

MOCK: I liked being watched by a woman on a silk sheet bed.

JOE: Have you ever been watched by a woman on a silk sheet bed?

MOCK: Once.

JOE: When?

MOCK: A while ago.

         [Pause.]

JOE: Was it good?

MOCK: It was good, Joe.

JOE: Who was the woman?

         [An expression on Mock's face suggests to us that he is evading the question.]

MOCK: I met her in a club.

JOE: What club?

MOCK: I don't know.

JOE: Was it in town?

MOCK: No, it was somewhere else.

JOE: Where?

MOCK: Somewhere good.

JOE: Good?

MOCK: Good. She took me somewhere good.

JOE: With silk sheets?

MOCK: With silk sheets.

JOE: Where you took off your trousers and folded them on a chair.

MOCK: No chair.

JOE: You left them on the floor.

MOCK: I did.

         [Pause.]

JOE: Were you still wearing your dicky bow, Mock?

MOCK: I wasn't wearing a dicky bow.

JOE: Then what were you wearing?

MOCK: I was naked. I was naked. I WAS NAKED.

JOE: Then you got on the bed?

MOCK: I did.

JOE: Was the woman wearing trousers, Mock?

MOCK: WHAT KIND OF WOMAN WOULD WEAR TROUSERS ON A SILK SHEET BED?

JOE: A WOMAN WHO DIDN'T KNOW WHO SHE WAS.

MOCK: SHE KNEW WHO SHE WAS.

JOE: AND SHE WASN'T WEARING TROUSERS?

MOCK: SHE WAS NAKED.

JOE: TWO NAKED BODIES ON A SILK SHEET BED.

MOCK: YES.

   [Pause.]

JOE: Who was she, Mock?

MOCK: I don't remember.

JOE: Was she beautiful?

MOCK: SHE WAS NAKED.

JOE: WAS SHE BEAUTIFUL?

MOCK: Questions, questions, questions, Joe, I don't re-member alright, I just don't remember.

JOE: I don't believe you, Mock.

MOCK: I don't care what you believe, it's the truth.

JOE: It's a lie.

MOCK: It's a truth.

JOE: You remembered the sheets.

MOCK: They have stuck in my mind.

JOE: Is your mind full of sheets?

MOCK: My mind is my mind.

JOE: And it's full of sheets of lies, the lying sheet of the mind.

MOCK: You don't know what you're talking about, Joe.

JOE: I do and you know I do.

MOCK: You're talking in a riddle.

JOE: I'M TALKING ABOUT DOTTY.

MOCK: DOTTY'S NOT HERE.

JOE: BUT SHE WAS THE WOMAN LYING NAKED ON A SILK SHEET BED.

MOCK: SHE WASN'T.

JOE: SHE WAS, MOCK, WAS.

MOCK: YOU'VE MADE IT UP.

JOE: I HAVEN'T MADE IT UP.

MOCK: YOUR IMAGINATION MAKING PICTURES.

JOE: THERE WERE NO PICTURES, IT'S THE TRUTH.

MOCK: DON'T FUCKING RATTLE ME, JOE.

JOE: YOU RATTLE BECAUSE I AM CLOSE TO THE TRUTH.

MOCK: LAY OFF ME, JOE.

JOE: I HEAR YOU RATTLING. I HAVE TOUCHED THE SWEET TRUTH!

MOCK: IT IS NOT THE TRUTH, JOE!

JOE: THEN WHAT IS THE TRUTH?

        [Pause.]

MOCK: SHE SAID SHE WOULD PAINT ME.

JOE: PAINT YOU!

MOCK: PAINT MY CRAFT IN OIL AND CANVAS.

JOE: What for?

MOCK: She said art can save culture.

JOE: What is culture?

MOCK: What is art?

JOE: What the fuck did Dotty tell you that for?

MOCK: BECAUSE SHE IS AN ARTIST.

JOE: I FUCKING HATE ART.

MOCK: You know nothing about it.

JOE: I know Van Gogh.

MOCK: What about him?

JOE: He chopped off his ear.

MOCK: So.

JOE: He was a Dutchman.

MOCK: So is Johann Cruyff.

JOE: Who's he?

MOCK: He was a footballer.

JOE: Van Gogh was an artist.

MOCK: So what are you saying?

JOE: Johann Cruyff never chopped his ear off.

MOCK: As far as you know.

JOE: I'VE FUCKING SEEN HIM ON TELLY, AND BOTH HIS EARS WERE INTACT.

MOCK: The telly tells lies.

JOE: I know what I saw.

MOCK: What has football got to do with art?

JOE: Football is art.

MOCK: Then why don't footballers chop off their ears?

JOE: How the fuck do I know?

MOCK: That is the question, Joe, that is the question.

JOE: What's the answer?

MOCK: VAN GOGH SHOULD HAVE BEEN A FOOT-BALLER.

JOE: Exactly.

MOCK: Like Cruyff.

JOE: Then he wouldn't have chopped off his ear.

MOCK: Van Gogh was born in the wrong age.

JOE: He was.

MOCK: Like me.

JOE: You're a crap footballer.

MOCK: I'm a good craftsman.

JOE: YOU'RE A GOOD BUTCHER.

MOCK: I AM NO BUTCHER, JOE! NO MAN IN THIS COUNTRY KILLS WITH MY SPEED AND SKILL. THE SKILL BREEDS THE SPEED, THE CRAFT, THE SWIFTNESS OF HAND, THE KEEN EDGE OF THE KNIFE THAT CUTS CLEANLY, QUIET-LY, WITHOUT PAIN, WITHOUT SUFFERING. I PAY THE BEASTS RESPECT, THEY DIE WITH DIGNITY, NOT ONE BEAST LEAVES THIS HOUSE WITHOUT A RESPECTABLE DEATH. NOT ONE.

JOE: A sheep is a sheep, a pig is a pig, they were all born ignorant. How can you respect a creature who gets excited by grass, that pisses and shits without thinking and stares with dull and vacant

143

eyes at a world he knows nothing about; the only reason I respect a bull in here is because of its horns, that if I lost my concentration and looked away I'd find embedded in my back or bowels or balls. They're all dull bastards I'm glad to see dead, NOW BUTCHER THE REMAINING LAMBS OR LET ME DO IT!

[Suddenly some rubbish comes clattering down to earth in a clutter of disintegrating music which reverberates and resonates throughout the scene. Joe rummages around in it. Mock looks frustrated.]

MOCK: JESUS CHRIST!

JOE: Fuck all but rubbish and a bottle of 'Fairy Liquid'. *[silence]* Mock? *[silence]* A bottle of 'Fairy Liquid,' Mock.

MOCK: Fuck your 'Fairy Liquid'.

JOE: It was the only good thing in the rubbish!

MOCK: FUCK ALL RUBBISH THAT FALLS DOWN FROM THE SKY ON MY HEAD, I WAS TALKING ABOUT ART.

[Mock throws it into the darkness.]

JOE: THERE WAS NO NEED TO THROW IT!

[Mock is just about to answer when there is a sound of a splash. They both freeze.]

MOCK: Did you hear what I heard?

JOE: I think I did.

MOCK: What did you hear?

JOE: A splash.

MOCK: Exactly.

JOE: Water.

MOCK: There must have been a flood.

JOE: I haven't heard.

MOCK: Nor me.

JOE: We would have heard.

MOCK: Jesus.

JOE: THIS IS A SLAUGHTER-HOUSE.

MOCK: NOT AN ISLAND.

JOE: Exactly.

MOCK: Throw something else.

JOE: Where?

MOCK: The other side, over there.

JOE: Into the darkness.

MOCK: Into the darkness.

JOE: I'm not sure I want to.

MOCK: It's the only way that we'll find out the truth.

[Joe thinks, picks up a can.]

JOE: Will a can do?

MOCK: It will do.

JOE: Then I'll throw a can.

MOCK: Good.

[Joe pulls back his arm, Mock watches intently, Joe stops.]

MOCK: What's the problem?

JOE: I don't know.

MOCK: What do you mean, you don't know?

JOE: I think I'm afraid.

MOCK: What do you mean you think you're afraid? You're either afraid or you're not.

JOE: I AM AFRAID.

MOCK: That's better.

JOE: I'M FUCKING AFRAID, MOCK.

MOCK: So am I.

JOE: Both of us stand here afraid.

[They both look around. Mock takes the can from Joe.]

JOE: What are you doing?

MOCK: I'm going to throw it.

JOE: I don't want you to throw it.

MOCK: Then go over there and cover your ears.

JOE: How will I do that?

MOCK: Turn on the radio or something.

JOE: Have we got a radio?

MOCK: I think one fell last Sunday.

JOE: Sunday?

MOCK: I think it was Sunday because I heard the singing of hymns.

JOE: That's no proof of anything, they could have been recorded.

MOCK: Do you think I don't know the difference between a recording and reality?

JOE: No.

MOCK: Well, you're wrong.

JOE: I'm right.

MOCK: No.

JOE: Yes.

MOCK: Lie.

JOE: Truth.

MOCK: Fiction.

JOE: Fact.

MOCK: Fantasy.

JOE: Reality.

MOCK: Bollocks.

JOE: What do you know?

MOCK: I know the difference between fantasy and reality.

JOE: Crap.

MOCK: Fantasy is imagination unrestricted by reality.

JOE: And reality?

MOCK: Is the state of things as they are, rather than how you might wish them to be.

JOE: How are things?

MOCK: Critical.

JOE: How do you know?

MOCK: I once read a dictionary from cover to cover then threw it away.

JOE: You threw it away! Why?

MOCK: Because it ended in Z.

JOE: What's wrong with Z?

MOCK: Nothing, but Z is where the known ends and the unknown begins.

JOE: The unknown is a dangerous place.

MOCK: It is.

JOE: It could be anywhere.

MOCK: Or anything.

JOE: Exactly, out there, all around.

        [Pause as they both look.]

JOE: I'm afraid, Mock.

MOCK: We're not alone in our fear.

JOE: No, there must be others.

MOCK: Yes.

JOE: But it doesn't make it any easier.

MOCK: No.

JOE: I don't know where we are, Mock.

MOCK: Neither do I.

JOE: I don't know who we are, Mock.

MOCK: I have a hunch.

JOE: A hunch!

MOCK: Yes.

JOE: Who are we then?

MOCK: I think you may be my brother.

JOE: BOLLOCKS.

MOCK: YOU COULD BE.

JOE: I WOULD HAVE KNOWN.

MOCK: HOW WOULD YOU KNOW?

JOE: I DON'T KNOW, BUT I WOULD KNOW.

MOCK: IT IS POSSIBLE, JOE.

JOE: IT IS IMPOSSIBLE.

MOCK: YOU DENY THE POSSIBILITY?

JOE: YES.

MOCK: THEN EXPLAIN THIS....

[Mock holds up Joe's dicky bow.]

JOE: That's my dicky bow.

MOCK: Yes, but it didn't come from Tom Jones, Joe.

JOE: It did.

MOCK: It didn't, this one is mine! It's the one I lost.

JOE: You never wore a dicky bow.

MOCK: Yes I did.

JOE: When then?

MOCK: I WAS ONCE A NIGHTCLUB BOUNCER IN A SMALL PROVINCIAL TOWN.

JOE: So?

MOCK: I opened the door one night and a man reached in and stole my dicky bow then ran away.

JOE: Lie.

MOCK: Truth.

JOE: Bollocks.

MOCK: HE JUMPED IN A TAXI, JOE!

[Pause.]

JOE: And you followed?

MOCK: I got into a taxi behind him and told the driver to "Follow that car!" and he did. He said it felt like being in a movie!

[Pause.]

My adrenalin was pumping, Joe, I could feel my pumping heart. We drove through the city at high speed, Joe, and reached the city limits, the driver turned round and said, "Do you want me to go on?" and I said, "Sure drive, you drive where you want to," and he said, "But we're in the middle of nowhere, man!"

[Pause.]

He said he was a stock-car racer, spent his weekends stock-car racing, said his girlfriend left him in the middle of a Sunday afternoon race, said he was angry about it but what could he do? I said it happens.

[Pause.]

I got out of the car, paid the fare and watched him drive away.

[Pause.]

I looked around and there was nothing. I looked down and there was grass, black grass, I looked up and saw the stars, bright stars. Then I looked around again, and I saw sheep.

[Pause.]

"Baaa...," said the sheep. "Baaa...," I said back.

[Pause.]

Then I heard a cough. I looked around, it was another sheep, standing still, staring at me, then another and another and another, the place was full of sheep, Joe. ME IN MY WHITE SHIRT, SHINY SHOES AND SMART SUIT, THE STARS ABOVE ME, THE SHEEP AROUND ME, THE SOUND OF WIND IN MY EARS AND I THOUGHT, WHY THE BLOODY HELL DOES A MAN LEAN IN AND STEAL MY DICKY BOW?

JOE: THERE ARE MILLIONS OF BLACK DICKY BOWS, MOCK.

MOCK: NOT ONES WITH 'MOCK' WRITTEN ON THE BACK.

JOE: WHAT?

MOCK: MOCK... M... O... C... K... MOCK!

JOE: THERE'S NO MOCK ON THIS.

MOCK: HAVE YOU LOOKED?

JOE: DO YOU THINK I DON'T KNOW MY OWN DICKY BOW?

MOCK: TAKE A LOOK, JOE.

JOE: No.

MOCK: Take a look, Joe.

[Joe takes his dicky bow and looks.]

MOCK: Well?

JOE: Nothing.

MOCK: Ink.

JOE: No Mock.

MOCK: But ink?

JOE: Yes, ink.

MOCK: It's Mock, faded with time.

JOE: Could be anything.

MOCK: Could be Mock.

JOE: Jesus.

MOCK: You could be my brother. My brother went East, and so did you.

JOE: I went to Saudi.

MOCK: You bought me a knife.

JOE: From a bedouin in the desert, but so what?

MOCK: My father said, "Your brother's gone East in search of the sun with a dicky bow round his neck."

JOE: Your father is dead.

MOCK: But I still remember what he said.

JOE: I never went to the desert with a dicky bow round

my neck.

MOCK: YOU STOLE MY DICKY BOW JOE AND YOU MAY BE MY BROTHER.

JOE: BOLLOCKS.

MOCK: TRUTH.

JOE: LIE.

MOCK: NO.

JOE: YES, MOCK, YES. I AM NOT YOUR BROTHER.

MOCK: I've got a hunch that you are.

JOE: A hunch?

MOCK: Yes, you know something because... you feel it.

JOE: I feel nothing.

MOCK: JESUS.

[Pause.]

JOE: Is there no other way of telling?

MOCK: There is but....

JOE: Something more reliable than a hunch.

MOCK: There must be.

JOE: BECAUSE MY HUNCHES ARE SOMETIMES SO UNRELIABLE.

MOCK: I took it for granted.

JOE: A mistake.

MOCK: I thought it was obvious.

JOE: Obviously not.

MOCK: What has happened to memory?

JOE: We forgot to remember.

MOCK: Remember what?

JOE: Who we are.

MOCK: WHO ARE WE?

JOE: My name is Joe, I salt the skins, I pull the chains, I put the head and feet in bins.

MOCK: And you may be my brother.

JOE: I don't think so, Mock.

MOCK: I want to be sure.

JOE: You can never be sure.

MOCK: I WANT SOLID GROUND.

JOE: You can't let the grass grow under your feet.

MOCK: What grass?

JOE: The green grass.

MOCK: What green grass?

JOE: The green, green grass.

MOCK: Of home.

JOE: What?

MOCK: Home.

JOE: Where?

MOCK: Here.

JOE: The green, green, grass of home?

MOCK: That's what I said.

JOE: This is home?

MOCK: Yes, we could have grown up here.

JOE: We could have moved.

MOCK: WHY IS IT SO FUCKING CONFUSING?

JOE: It's the way it is.

MOCK: WHERE THE FUCK IS MY YOUTH?

JOE: Youth?

MOCK: The first twenty years.

JOE: Must be locked in your head.

MOCK: My head is injured.

JOE: I tried to protect it.

MOCK: Protect it from what?

JOE: The wall. You were sleep-walking, you were smashing your head against the cold white wall, you were hurting yourself. I am a light sleeper. I woke up, I stopped you, you wouldn't stop, you wouldn't wake up. You kept shouting and shouting. "Shame," you shouted, "shame, shame, shame."

MOCK: I never woke up?

JOE: I pulled you away, your eyes were open but they were dulled and glazed, you had a lump on your head, I put you in chains, I thought you were dead.

MOCK: I AM NOT DEAD.

JOE: I tried to protect you, you were hurting yourself. What could I do?

MOCK: You should have woken me.

JOE: You were asleep.

MOCK: I WAKE DON'T I? YOU'VE SEEN ME AWAKE?

JOE: You were in a coma.

MOCK: You should have roused me.

JOE: You were unconscious.

MOCK: Then when did I wake?

JOE: What?

MOCK: WHEN DID I WAKE?

JOE: I DON'T KNOW.

MOCK: COULD BE DAYS.

JOE: MONTHS.

MOCK: YEARS! AM I AWAKE, JOE?

JOE: I DON'T FUCKING KNOW.

MOCK: AM I YOUR BROTHER?

JOE: HOW THE FUCK SHOULD I KNOW?

MOCK: YOU KNOW BECAUSE YOU KNOW.

JOE: I KNOW FUCK ALL.

MOCK: THEN WHAT THE FUCK HAS GONE WRONG WITH THE WORLD?

[Sudden harsh, discordant music as objects come crashing down from above. Mock and Joe scream and take cover. Lights fade to darkness. Silence.]

MOCK: *[in darkness]* We're drowning.

[Pause. Lights up on Mock.]

I can feel the water rise over my knees, thighs, stomach, neck. I'm up to my neck in the blood red sea, skin, steel and bone. Is it a sea of blood or is the blood sea?

[Pause.]

I am tired. There is no opposition in me, no tension, only thoughts, perhaps thoughts of a thousand hopes, a thousand fears clashing. A war of thoughts in my drowning mind. Am I suffocating memory? Am I suffocating myself? Am I already dead?

[Pause.]

Must break the silence, speak... speak... SPEAK... SPEAK...

[Mock weeps. An alarm bell sounds, lights come up, Joe looks at an exhausted Mock and smiles before springing into action, hoisting up a corpse on chains. Joe counts.]

JOE: 35, 36, 37, 38, 39, 40.

MOCK: Count them again.

JOE: There's no need to count them again.

MOCK: Forty?

JOE: Yes.

[Pause.]

MOCK: I can't kill any more, Joe.

JOE: I know.

MOCK: I have reached my daily capacity.

JOE: You have, so give me your knife.

MOCK: NO.

JOE: YES.

MOCK: NO.

JOE: YES, FUCKING YES, FUCKING YES, YES, YES.

MOCK: STAY AWAY FROM ME, JOE. This house has no room for two craftsmen. We would compete, the competition would lead to a race, the race makes us tired, we would get sloppy, sloppy work is dangerous, accidents will happen.

[During the next exchange, Joe gradually begins to dominate Mock, verbally and physically in a macabre exhausting dance to submission.]

JOE: I don't care about accidents, I don't care about craftsmanship, sheep, people or beasts, I care about fuck all, I JUST FEEL LIKE KILLING, THAT'S ALL.

MOCK: YOU SHALL NOT KILL, JOE.

JOE: Why not.

MOCK: Because there is a difference between us, I see the mystery where you see only ignorance.

JOE: I AM NOT IGNORANT.

MOCK: You don't respect the beasts, Joe.

JOE: THEY ARE NOT WORTHY OF RESPECT.

MOCK: You don't see the mystery.

JOE: WHAT FUCKING MYSTERY?

MOCK: The mystery in their eyes, before they go from flesh to fuck all, the mystery that lies in their fearful heads, in the quartered flesh, the twitching nerve, the broken bones. There is a mystery to this world, Joe, that I am afraid of, that I must respect.

JOE: BOLLOCKS, ABSOLUTE BOLLOCKS.

MOCK: IT IS NOT BOLLOCKS.

JOE: There is no mystery, Mock.

MOCK: There is because I see it, I fear it.

JOE: You fear guilt, you bury your guilt in the blood that you spill. YOU CALL IT A MYSTERY BE-CAUSE IT IS A VEIL THAT HIDES THE BOOT OF SHAME THAT STINGS OUR FACE AND RIBS!

MOCK: NO.

JOE: YES.

MOCK: NO.

JOE: YES, YES, YES! THEY DID NOT ASK TO BE KILLED!

MOCK: I HONOUR THE BEAST, I SAW THE MYSTERY THEREFORE I AM ABSOLVED OF BLAME, ABSOLVED OF GUILT, I AM FUCKING INNO-CENT.

JOE: YOU ARE NOT INNOCENT, NONE OF US ARE INNOCENT.

MOCK: I KILL WITH DIGNITY!

JOE: THERE IS NO DIGNITY, MOCK, WE HAVE LOST OUR DIGNITY, WE ARE NO LONGER WORTHY OF HONOUR. WE LIVE IN SHAME, IT IS AN AGE OF SHAME.

[Pause.]

MOCK: Then I live in the wrong age.

JOE: You are not a man of these times, I'll admit.

MOCK: I hate these times.

JOE: You are not the only one, but either you adapt, or....

MOCK: What?

JOE: You will be crushed.

MOCK: No.

JOE: Yes.

MOCK: No.

JOE: Yes.

MOCK: I WILL NOT LIVE IN SHAME, JOE.

JOE: You've got no choice.

MOCK: I MUST HAVE A CHOICE.

JOE: You haven't got a choice.

MOCK: What happened to choice?

JOE: It fucked off when we needed it most.

MOCK: And now it's too late?

JOE: Course it is, we've shot our fucking bolt.

MOCK: So what do we do, go with the flow?

JOE: We've got to.

MOCK: Like two headless chickens?

JOE: Cock-a-doodle-doo and cockle doodle doo.

MOCK: To the end.

JOE: ALL THE WAY, MOCK, ALL THE WAY, ROUND THE HOUSES, DOWN THE CHIMNEY. UP IN SMOKE, FOLLOW THE FLOW TILL....

MOCK: THE WHOLE FUCKING SHIT PALACE FALLS ON OUR HEADS.

JOE: BINGO! BINGO! BINGO! HE WINS ALL THE SILVER IN TOWN. COLLECT. COLLECT.

MOCK: No.

JOE: What do you mean, no?

MOCK: We won't let it happen.

JOE: It's already happened.

MOCK: Not to me it hasn't.

JOE: Jesus Christ.

MOCK: I WILL STILL KILL WITH DIGNITY.

JOE: WHO THE FUCK DO YOU THINK YOU ARE?

MOCK: Mock Alone, I'm a killer of beasts.

JOE: Then why won't you kill him and all the sheep that remain?

MOCK: I am not the only one asking questions, there must be others who lurk.

JOE: IN A BAG OF IGNORANCE.

MOCK: WE ARE NOT IN A BAG OF IGNORANCE.

JOE: OF COURSE WE FUCKING ARE. WE FOLLOW-ED. WE DID THE FOLLOWING. THE PIPER PLAYED HIS TUNE AND WE COCK-A-DOOD-

LE-DOOD. WE FOLLOWED THE BUGLE OF SWEET GENERAL GOOD!

MOCK: WE SHOULD NOT HAVE FOLLOWED.

JOE: We are the hungry chicks of defeat, Mock, the waiting dodos, the soon to be extinct. We are insignificant, ignored, afraid, silent and forgotten. WE ARE THE LAST PLACE.

MOCK: What you mean?

JOE: We have shrunk.

MOCK: Shrunk?

JOE: Shrunk, we are less than we used to be and getting less every day.

MOCK: Explain.

JOE: I can't.

MOCK: Why not?

JOE: It's difficult.

MOCK: Try me.

JOE: WE ARE NOT WHAT WE SHOULD BE!

MOCK: We are dying?

JOE: Yes.

MOCK: JESUS.

JOE: It's horrible.

MOCK: Fantastic.

JOE: It is fucking monstrous.

MOCK: WE MUST ACT.

JOE: How act?

MOCK: DEFY.

JOE: There is no defiance.

MOCK: NOT SUBMIT.

JOE: We live in submission.

MOCK: WE MUST NOT FALL.

JOE: WE HAVE ALREADY FALLEN.

MOCK: I HAVE NOT FALLEN.

JOE: You have.

MOCK: I haven't.

JOE: I KNOW WHAT I SEE.

MOCK: What do you see?

JOE: Look for yourself.

MOCK: I know what I look like.

JOE: Then look again!

MOCK: Nothing.

JOE: There is....

MOCK: It's me, my head, my teeth, my nose, my eyes, my ears, my hair.

JOE: It's not how it used to be.

MOCK: It is.

JOE: It's not.

MOCK: I have aged that's all.

JOE: Look at your eyes.

MOCK: Clear.

JOE: Not as clear as they used to be.

MOCK: THAT MAN IS ME AND I HAVE NOT FALLEN.

JOE: You are falling and you know you are.

MOCK: NO.

JOE: YES.

MOCK:	NO, NO, NO.
JOE:	THEN LIVE IN DELUSION!
MOCK:	What's in my eyes, Joe?
JOE:	Nothing, as you say.
MOCK:	What's in my eyes, Joe? What can you see?
JOE:	You won't listen if I tell you.
MOCK:	I will listen, I want you to tell me.
JOE:	YOUR SOUL IS IN DECAY.
MOCK:	NO.
JOE:	ALL SOULS ARE IN DECAY.
MOCK:	NOT MINE I....
JOE:	WE ARE ALL SOULS OF THE LATE TWENT-IETH CENTURY AND THEY CAN ONLY BE IN DECAY.
MOCK:	I AM NOT A MAN OF THESE TIMES, YOU SAID SO YOURSELF. I STILL HAVE NOT LOST FAITH!
JOE:	FAITH? THERE IS NO FAITH.
MOCK:	I WILL NOT SUBMIT.
JOE:	WE HAVE ALREADY SUBMITTED.
MOCK:	I WILL FIND A SOLUTION, WRESTLE FOR AN ANSWER!
JOE:	IT IS IMPOSSIBLE! WE ARE AN EXCITED HORSE WHO'S UNSEATED HIS JOCKEY RUNN-ING HEADLONG INTO A VOID.
MOCK:	A WHAT?
JOE:	A BOTTOMLESS PIT.
MOCK:	A BRICK WALL?
JOE:	THE END. OBLIVION.

MOCK: CATASTROPHE, JOE.

JOE: EXACTLY, WE'LL SHOOT THE HORSE!

MOCK: WHAT?

JOE: PUT IT OUT OF ITS MISERY.

MOCK: WE CAN'T SHOOT THE HORSE.

JOE: WHY NOT? IF IT'S AIMLESS AND EXCITED IT'S...

MOCK: WE ARE THE FUCKING HORSE.

JOE: A CAREERING HORSE IS A CAREERING HORSE.

MOCK: THEN WE'LL FIND IT A JOCKEY!

JOE: A JOCKEY?

MOCK: YES, YES.

JOE: ARE YOU MAD?

MOCK: WE'LL FIND A JOCKEY, MANY JOCKEYS, ME AND YOU.

JOE: JESUS CHRIST. *[laughing]*

MOCK: WHY ARE YOU LAUGHING?

JOE: IT'S MORE HOPELESS THAN I THOUGHT.

MOCK: WHAT'S WRONG, JOE?

JOE: IT'S BOLLOCKS.

MOCK: IT'S NOT BOLLOCKS!

JOE: IT'S HOPELESS.

MOCK: IT IS NOT HOPELESS.

JOE: YOU, ME, US, JESUS!

MOCK: WHAT ABOUT US, WE ARE MAKING....

JOE: A METAPHOR.

MOCK: A WHAT?

JOE: WE HAVE MADE ONLY A METAPHOR, A BAD METAPHOR.

MOCK: IT HAS GIVEN US A START.

JOE: WHAT START?

MOCK: THE START OF THE SOLUTION.

JOE: IT HAS GIVEN US NOTHING, WORDS, AVOID-ANCE, EVASION, SHEER ORNAMENTATION.

MOCK: WE HAVE NOT AVOIDED.

JOE: IT'S IN THE HEAD, EVASION, LIFE IS OUT OF HERE.

MOCK: DON'T YOU THINK I KNOW THAT?

JOE: I DON'T KNOW WHAT YOU KNOW.

MOCK: I KNOW WHAT I KNOW.

JOE: YOU ARE DELUDED.

MOCK: KNOWLEDGE IS POWER.

JOE: THEN WHY AREN'T YOU POWERFUL?

MOCK: I AM.

JOE: YOU'RE NOT.

MOCK: I AM.

JOE: YOU'RE NOT.

MOCK: NEITHER ARE YOU.

JOE: I KNOW.

MOCK: HOW'S THAT?

JOE: I WAS MISINFORMED.

MOCK: BY WHO?

JOE: THE POWERS THAT BE.

MOCK: MISINFORMATION IS NO PATH TO KNOW-LEDGE.

JOE: I KNOW.

MOCK: SO WHAT ARE YOU SAYING?

JOE: I BELIEVED MISINFORMATION, I BELIEVED THE MESSAGE.

MOCK: WHAT WAS THE MESSAGE?

JOE: THAT WE ARE PROGRESSING.

MOCK: WE ARE NOT.

JOE: NO, WE'RE FUCKED.

MOCK: YOU SHOULDN'T HAVE LISTENED TO THE MESSAGE, IT MADE YOU A COCKLE, A COCK-A-DOODLE-DOO.

JOE: I FOLLOWED THE CROWD.

MOCK: THE HERD.

JOE: THE MEEK.

MOCK: THE SERVILE.

JOE: THE SHAMED. I LIVE IN SHAME.

MOCK: I DON'T.

JOE: YOU DO.

MOCK: I NEVER FOLLOWED.

JOE: YOU DID.

MOCK: PROVE IT.

JOE: YOU ARE IN CRISIS, YOU ARE THE SAME AS EVERYONE ELSE.

MOCK: NO... NO... NO.

[He collapses in submission, exhausted. Joe laughs, seizes his opportunity and to the accompaniment of drums and music, begins to beat Mock mercilessly, and

*eventually drags him to a chain where he hoists Mock
up like a carcass. Music fades. Lights fade to darkness.]*

*[In darkness giving way to dawn light, which reveals
Joe speaking on a telephone as Mock hangs.]*

JOE: I did tell him see, Mr Cragg. I said, "Mock," I said,
"don't come in with the forty a day as a daily
capacity to me because I won't buy it". We are
stock loading sheep as if there was no tomorrow.

[Pause.]

Oh don't worry, Mr Cragg, I'll kill as many as you
need, I'm the main man now, Mr Cragg.

[Pause.]

Yes, goodbye, Mr Cragg, and thanks.

*[Joe puts down the phone. He sharpens a knife with a
steel. He turns on some bland music on the radio. He
moves over to Mock, who suddenly opens his eyes and
stops Joe in his tracks.]*

MOCK: I'm still here, Joe.

*[Joe says nothing, just stares at Mock. Music fades,
lights fade as a painting of a woman dancing on a red
sea can be seen hanging above the set.]*

I AM STILL HERE.

*[Lights fade on the set, and then on the hanging
painting to darkness.]*

FINISH

East From The Gantry

Notes to the Original Production

East From The Gantry was first performed at Tramway, Glasgow on 10 October, 1992 and published by Methuen in July, 1993. This new, revised version of the play was performed at Chapter Arts Centre, Cardiff on 2 February, 1994.

Cast

Trampas..Richard Lynch
Bella...Ri Richards
Ronnie..Boyd Clack

Directed by..Edward Thomas
Lighting by.......................................Nick MacLiammoir
Set by...............Ian Buchanan and Nick MacLiammoir
(based on an original idea by Ian Hill)
Songs by....................Boyd Clack and Clive Trevelyan
Music Written and Performed by.......Gareth Whittock

Start

[A derelict house on a mountain surrounded by snow. A blue moon lights up the sky. The remains of a long ago feast may litter a table; candles may add extra light. Trampas smokes, Bella looks eastwards.]

TRAMPAS: It was a Sunday night. There'd been some flooding down the valley, Uncle Jim had gone to see the damage for himself. Liked disasters did my Uncle Jim, my mother told me not to be too hard on him because of the trauma he suffered as a boy. She was still in her cot when it happened, Uncle Jim was ten and my Uncle Ieu was fourteen.

BELLA: Fourteen is a difficult age.

TRAMPAS: My grandmother was making breakfast when Ieu picked up a loaded shotgun and shot her dead with both barrels. It was an accident, he didn't know it was loaded, but it affected him and Uncle Jim, they were never the same again.

BELLA: That's terrible.

TRAMPAS: When he was out watching the valley flood, my mother turned to me just as Fred Housego, the taxi driver, was winning 'Mastermind'. "Can I let you into a secret?" she said. And I said "Sure thing ma, what's on your mind?", "I'm in love with him," she said. "With Fred Housego?" I said. "No," she said, "with Magnus Magnusson."

BELLA: Get away.

TRAMPAS: It's the truth, she said she'd written him hundreds of letters.

BELLA: Did he ever reply?

TRAMPAS: Not personally, no, just a note from his office saying best wishes and a signed photo. She was very disappointed.

BELLA: I can imagine.

TRAMPAS: She was gutted.

BELLA: I bet.

TRAMPAS: She always thought she'd meet him somewhere see, perhaps share a drink in front of the fire, chew the cud. She thought Magnus would have told her fantastic tales of old Iceland long into the night.

BELLA: She sounds a very nice person.

TRAMPAS: She was. She got me to hire a sailing boat once, with a European skipper, to take us to Iceland but we got lost in heavy fog off the Scottish coast and had to turn back.

BELLA: That's a pity.

TRAMPAS: I suppose it is.

BELLA: They say Reykjavik's a really interesting place.

TRAMPAS: Really?

BELLA: Yes.

TRAMPAS: Have you ever been there?

BELLA: No. I just read about it once.

TRAMPAS: Oh. [pause] She died not long after that on the same day I saw Telly Savalas window shopping in the city. I was on the bus stuck in traffic, just staring out of the window, when bingo, there he was, bald head, dark glasses, lollipop in his mouth, dark trousers and canary yellow shoes. I jumped out of my seat, taking a pen and an unpaid gas bill out of my pocket for an autograph and ran downstairs. I had to move fast, Telly was making his way to a smart black limo parked on double-yellows with a chauffeur holding onto the door. With my eyes fixed firmly on my prize, I stepped off the bus and smash, collided with an Australian cycle messenger, overtaking on the inside, who knocked me senseless to the floor.

BELLA: And Telly?

TRAMPAS: By the time I came round, Telly and the cyclist and everyone else was gone. When I got back to Johnny Greco's I got a phone call from Uncle Jim, saying I had to come home straight away because my mother wasn't well. "But I've just seen Telly Savalas in the street," I said. "Did you get his autograph?" asked Uncle Jim. "No" I said, "I..." but before I had time to explain, Uncle Jim called me a stupid git and put down the phone and that was that.

BELLA: How insensitive can you get?

TRAMPAS: Exactly, I was gutted, when I got home I found Uncle Jim sitting with Mam looking sheepish. She was looking up at the ceiling with a Turkish Delight on her chest, Uncle Jim said she'd been dead for two hours, but it was very peaceful.

BELLA: It must have been a shock.

TRAMPAS: It was. *[pause]* I loved her, I really loved her.

[Trampas begins to break down. Bella rummages around in her bag. She pulls out an apple and offers it to him.]

BELLA: I'm sorry.

TRAMPAS: Forget it.

RONNIE: Bella?

[Lights and music change as Trampas moves into the shadows and Ronnie enters holding a gun to his head.

Bella throws pieces of paper from her bag into the air and laughs at him. Ronnie gets exasperated.]

RONNIE: BELLA!

BELLA: Can't you see I'm thinking.

RONNIE: With paper?

BELLA: My mind is scrambled, my thoughts are scattered, my brain is fragmented to fuck.

RONNIE: That's because you're drunk.

BELLA: *[throwing paper at him]* I am not fucking DRUNK, Ron.

RONNIE: Don't you throw paper at me.

BELLA: It's my paper.

RONNIE: How do I know that?

BELLA: Look for yourself.

RONNIE: I'm not going to get down on my hands and knees to do that.

BELLA: Here then, look have one from my bag.

[Ronnie takes it, looks at it.]

RONNIE: This isn't my handwriting. Whose handwriting is this?

BELLA: What?

RONNIE: This isn't yours, Bella.

BELLA: It is.

RONNIE: It's not. Your handwriting slopes backwards.

BELLA: Let me see.

RONNIE: It says "I love...." Who the fuck's been writing you love letters, Bella?

BELLA: You don't think...?

RONNIE: You could have....

BELLA: Oh come on.

RONNIE: You're capable of anything when you're drunk.

BELLA: I'm not drunk, Ronnie, smell my breath.

RONNIE: Pooh... whiskey.

BELLA: Bollocks. It's definitely not whiskey, you know I don't drink whiskey.

RONNIE: Rum then, rum, it's definitely rum.

BELLA: I had a tipple, that's all.

RONNIE: You're drunk, Bella.

BELLA: No way.

RONNIE: Prove it.

BELLA: I'm not going to prove it to you. Why should I?

RONNIE: Here we go again, looking to start something, bit of a bundle, shot in the dark.

BELLA: You're deliberately provoking me.

RONNIE: Walk the line.

BELLA: What?

RONNIE: If you're not fucking drunk, fucking walk.

BELLA: You bastard, I....

RONNIE: THE LINE, THE LINE. WALK THE LINE!

BELLA: What line?

RONNIE: That line over there will do.

BELLA: I don't see it.

RONNIE: It's covered in crap, that's why.

BELLA: It's your crap.

RONNIE: You put it there.

BELLA: I was tidying up, that's all.

RONNIE: Is that what you call it?

BELLA: Yes, I tidy as much as you.

RONNIE: Crap.

BELLA: I defrosted the fridge, Ronnie.

RONNIE: I did it both times before that.

BELLA: Impossible. We haven't had it that long.

RONNIE: It didn't defrost by itself, Bella.

BELLA: I know.

RONNIE: So what are you saying?

BELLA: I'm saying it's come to something when a man asks his wife to walk the fucking line for him.

RONNIE: It's a point of principle, Bella.

BELLA: I will not walk the line, Ron.

RONNIE: Not ever?

BELLA: No.

RONNIE: Not even in the interests of truth?

BELLA: Not in this case, no.

RONNIE: This is very disappointing, Bella, truth is the cornerstone of marriage.

BELLA: I'm telling you truthfully that I am not drunk, Ron.

RONNIE: I'd like to believe you, but I'm afraid I just can't, Bella.

BELLA: This is sad, Ron, this is really sad.

          [Both of them looking into the wilderness.]

RONNIE: I know.

BELLA: You realise what this could mean?

[Pause.]

RONNIE: I do. Have you got an apple?

BELLA: An apple? What for?

RONNIE: To place on my head, after which you can take my shotgun, stand twelve paces away and shoot.

BELLA: Shoot what?

RONNIE: The apple, woman, the apple.

BELLA: And if I miss?

RONNIE: Then it proves you are drunk.

BELLA: But....

RONNIE: No buts, Bella, this is important.

BELLA: You are prepared to risk your life in order to prove to me I'm not drunk.

RONNIE: Yes.

BELLA: Then I'm sorry.

RONNIE: For what?

BELLA: I won't do it.

RONNIE: You must, Bella, you must.

BELLA: I have only had one shot of rum, Ron, now why won't you believe me?

RONNIE: Because, Bella, I am after a higher truth.

BELLA: *[aiming the gun at him]* But I'm a lousy shot.

RONNIE: It's something I've already taken into account, Bella, but I think your love for me will bring you through.

BELLA: Love doesn't always shoot straight, Ronnie, look what happened to William Burroughs.

RONNIE: Will you please not mention William Burroughs when contemplating shooting an apple off your spouse's head?

BELLA: But it's very relevant to the case, Ron.

RONNIE: William Burroughs was drunk, doped and crazy when he tried it and so by all accounts was his wife, now either confirm that you are as well or continue with the test.

BELLA: I am neither drunk, doped or crazy and you know it.

RONNIE: Then let's hope you won't William Burroughs me. Now fetch me an apple.

[Bella laughs.]

BELLA: There's no apple.

RONNIE: What?

BELLA: There's no apple, Ron.

RONNIE: I don't believe you, Bella, you always carry apples in your bag. You have a well-documented phobia of dentists.

BELLA: I ate my last one only this morning. We need to go into town to get more supplies.

RONNIE: Show me your bag.

BELLA: I can't.

RONNIE: You must.

BELLA: Impossible.

RONNIE: Don't get obstinate with me, Bella, this is not time for obstinacy, now pass me your bag.

BELLA: No, you can't. I don't want you looking in my bag, it's private.

RONNIE: There are no secrets between a husband and wife, Bella.

BELLA: I know but this is a question of my preferring my

independence, Ronnie.

RONNIE: If your independence stands between me and your bag then God help this marriage, that's what I say.

BELLA: You're missing the point altogether, Ronnie.

RONNIE: Okay, okay, have it your way, fuck the apple, fuck truth.

BELLA: *[laughing]* Ronnie.

RONNIE: Fuck William Burroughs, fuck marriage, fuck trust, long live INDEPENDENCE. SHAG THE WORLD.

BELLA: YOU ARE BEING COMPLETELY IRRATIONAL.

RONNIE: I don't know what else to say, Bella, but I'm gutted, you hear me, gutted. I've worked hard at our relationship as you well know, fraught as it's been with difficulties from the beginning. I have struggled to keep house and home together, endeavoured to keep our waning spirits high, while all you can do is stare at ceilings, rip up paper, deny me your most intimate secrets and fucking drink yourself stupid.

BELLA: So would you if you had been married to a trigger happy has-been, who, if he isn't sitting in a corner, is basically blowing the brains out of neighbouring townsfolk's domestic pets. *[uncovering a dead cat from the bag]*

RONNIE: I never meant to shoot that cat, Bella, it was an accident, I....

[Sudden sound of a ringing phone, fade in music as the lights change. Ronnie and Bella look warily around them.]

RONNIE: It's the phone.

BELLA: I know.

RONNIE: Are you expecting a call?

BELLA: No. Are you?

RONNIE: No. *[pause]*

BELLA: I think we should answer it.

RONNIE: No.

BELLA: Why not?

RONNIE: It might be a crazy bastard. I hate crazy bastards.

BELLA: You're a crazy bastard.

RONNIE: You think so?

BELLA: I do.

RONNIE: That's interesting.

           [Pause.]

BELLA: I'm going to answer it.

RONNIE: No, let me, it may be obscene.

BELLA: So.

RONNIE: I don't want you taking obscene calls, remember your pain is my pain, your perversion, my perversion.

BELLA: I'm a grown woman, I can handle it.

RONNIE: No.

           [Bella picks up the phone quickly. Music fades.]

BELLA: Hello? *[pause]* Did we order a pizza?

RONNIE: A pizza?

BELLA: A dish of Italian origin consisting of a baked disc of dough covered with cheese and tomatoes, usually with the addition of mushroom, anchovies, sausage or ham.

RONNIE: No.

BELLA: This woman says we did.

RONNIE: We can't have. You know I hate anchovies.

BELLA: You don't hate anchovies.

RONNIE: I do, ever since that sea-food platter in Sorrento.

BELLA: Sorrento?

RONNIE: A port in southwest Italy, between the bay of Naples and the gulf of Palermo, we spent our honeymoon there.

[Ronnie grabs Bella and starts to dance.]

BELLA: We went to Sorrento on our honeymoon?

RONNIE: Of course we did, Bella, we stayed in the Settimo Cielo! They double-booked. We spent our first night in a windowless room hewn from the rock next to an Italian couple with a wailing child.

BELLA: Ricardo!

RONNIE: That's the one.

BELLA: And that's the last time you ate an anchovy?

RONNIE: Yes.

BELLA: Jesus.

RONNIE: Tell her we'll have the pizza with artichoke instead of anchovy.

BELLA: Hello? Yes we'll have a thin crust ten-inch pizza with artichoke instead of anchovy. *[pause]* No artichoke.

RONNIE: No artichoke? What sort of pizza joint is this?

BELLA: Don't argue Ronnie, what else do you want with it?

RONNIE: Tell her we'll have pepperoni.

BELLA: Pepperoni? Good... how long will it be? Good. *[pause]* Do you want garlic bread with it?

RONNIE: No, do you?

BELLA: No. Soft drink?

RONNIE: Two soft drinks.

BELLA: We'll have two soft drinks, thanks.

            [She puts the phone down.]

RONNIE: I don't remember ordering a pizza, do you?

BELLA: No.

RONNIE: That's strange.

BELLA: It is, but I suppose it's a strange and weird world out there, Ronnie.

RONNIE: I know.

            [Fade in music of the sixties Western series 'The Virginian' as Ronnie exits and Trampas enters.]

BELLA: My name is Bella.

TRAMPAS: Pleased to meet you, Bella.

BELLA: And you?

TRAMPAS: Trampas.

BELLA: That's a funny name.

TRAMPAS: From 'The Virginian'.

BELLA: The Western series.

TRAMPAS: Yeah.

BELLA: 6:55 till 8:00 on a Friday night.

TRAMPAS: Bingo.

BELLA: Me and my brother used to watch that regular.

TRAMPAS: So did I.

BELLA: Instead of 'Bonanza'.

TRAMPAS: I never watched 'Bonanza'. Not when 'The Virginian' was on.

BELLA: I suppose not.

TRAMPAS: Trampas had a brown horse with a white patch.

BELLA: Trampas was a drifter.

TRAMPAS: Trampas was a good cowboy, ma'am.

BELLA: You called me ma'am.

TRAMPAS: Pardon me?

BELLA: Ma'am. You said ma'am.

TRAMPAS: Did I?

BELLA: Yes.

TRAMPAS: I'm sorry.

BELLA: I'm no ma'am, mister.

TRAMPAS: No, I know, it slipped out. What I mean is, I didn't mean to... I... it was a mistake. It's been a long time.

BELLA: What has?

TRAMPAS: I'm sorry.

BELLA: It's a funny thing to say.

TRAMPAS: I know.

BELLA: In a derelict house.

TRAMPAS: Yes.

BELLA: In the middle of winter.

TRAMPAS: Yes. I'm an idiot.

BELLA: It's strange.

TRAMPAS: Need my head read.

BELLA: Weird even.

TRAMPAS: I don't know what came over me.

BELLA: Because I mean, it's not as if we were in Wyoming, is it?

TRAMPAS: No.

BELLA: Or Iowa.

TRAMPAS: Dakota.

BELLA: Minnesota.

TRAMPAS: Utah.

BELLA: Or any other mid-western American state.

TRAMPAS: Exactly.

BELLA: We're in southern Powys.

TRAMPAS: Yes.

BELLA: In Wales.

TRAMPAS: Yes, Wales.

BELLA: A country.

TRAMPAS: On the west coast of Great Britain.

BELLA: Conquered in 1282.

TRAMPAS: Is it really that long ago?

BELLA: It certainly is.

TRAMPAS: Wow.

BELLA: Its economy is mainly agricultural.

TRAMPAS: Mainly, yes, but with an old industrial area down here in the south.

BELLA: Yes.

TRAMPAS: And old quarries and stuff in the north.

BELLA: With holiday destinations.

TRAMPAS: And holiday makers.

BELLA: Places to eat.

TRAMPAS: Yeah? Eat what?

BELLA: New season lamb on a Sunday with mint sauce,

buttered new potatoes, honey-glazed carrots...

TRAMPAS: ...Cut into rings not strips!

BELLA: With cabbage and a little gravy, followed by...

TRAMPAS: ...Home-made rice pudding with the skin on top!

[They laugh.]

BELLA: Afterwards we sit down together with coffee and chocolates.

TRAMPAS: Yes!

BELLA: Sometimes on summer afternoons, we go west as a family with children, parents and grandchildren in search of an afternoon tea, hoping to find a secluded farm house free of the Lambrettas and two-strokes with which our youths used to express their manly development.

TRAMPAS: I never express my manly development with a Lambretta, ma'am.

BELLA: Please don't call me ma'am.

TRAMPAS: I'm sorry.

BELLA: Forget it. *[pause]* Plenty of space here see, mister.

TRAMPAS: There is.

BELLA: I can see for miles.

TRAMPAS: Could be a good place in the right hands.

BELLA: With these hands.

TRAMPAS: I will cling to you.

BELLA: TOM JONES.

TRAMPAS: A legend.

BELLA: I used to think so, but not any more.

TRAMPAS: Why's that?

BELLA: I threw a pair of my best French underwear at him

in a concert in Swansea, but he never noticed.

TRAMPAS: No.

BELLA: Yes.

TRAMPAS: That's a shame.

BELLA: That's what I thought. I'm sorry I didn't throw him a pair of cheap, ordinary ones now.

TRAMPAS: Or not bothered at all.

BELLA: Exactly. It affected me badly that did. Made me lose a lot of self-confidence.

TRAMPAS: Superstars, even legends, can be so thoughtless sometimes, so unpredictable.

BELLA: I know. It was only a few days after that that I met my husband, Ronnie.

[Fade in music. Lights change. Ronnie enters and stands looking eastwards.]

BELLA: It was a Saturday afternoon. It was raining. I was watching greyhounds chase a fake rabbit round a track in the name of sport on TV. I'd just had a bath. I felt warm and good. I felt horny. I dreamt I was in a hotel room with Martin Bratton in a large bed, champagne, sex, heat. He was stroking my breasts with long, delicate fingers and kissing the back of my neck. I could feel the heat from the inside of his thigh and his breathing heavy. I wanted to fuck him there and then, on the bed, on the floor, on a chair, crazy, biting, clawing his back, making me come, again and again and again. *[pause]* But I was alone in my room, with the rain and the greyhounds, the fake bunnies and a phone. I picked up the phone book and flicked through the pages. I picked a number, any number at random. I lit a cigarette, and dialled.

[Ronnie walks to the other part of the stage and continues.]

RONNIE: I had some money on the 3:40 race, number 5, 'Brief Encounter'; he came fourth after leading for three quarters of the race. I felt empty and cheated, my mother said I was a fool for wasting my money. I was about to take her up on this when the phone rang. I don't know why, but I decided to answer it upstairs.

RONNIE: *[on phone]* 278063... hello?

BELLA: Can you say that again?

RONNIE: Sorry?

BELLA: What's the number again?

RONNIE: What number do you want?

BELLA: 278063.

RONNIE: This is 278063, who's calling? *[pause]* Hello?

BELLA: Bella, my name is Bella.

RONNIE: Bella.

BELLA: Bella... Who am I speaking to?

RONNIE: My name is Ron, Ron John, but if you don't mind I'd rather you called me Ronnie.

BELLA: Ronnie?

RONNIE: Yes. Ronnie.

BELLA: I've just come in, I've been shopping. There was a note on the table by the phone with this number on it. It said I should ring it.

RONNIE: I haven't spoken to anyone today. I'm sure I haven't... there must be a mistake.

BELLA: Do you think so?

RONNIE: Probably didn't write the right number down.

BELLA: Yes... yes... that's probably it... well I'm sorry to bother you. I didn't mean to take up your time.

RONNIE: Don't worry... it's just a mistake.

BELLA: I....

RONNIE: Can I ask you a question, please?

BELLA: If you like.

RONNIE: Are you... dressed? *[pause]* I'm sorry.

BELLA: I didn't hear what you said.

RONNIE: Oh. *[pause]* I asked... if you had... any clothes on. *[pause]* Bella?

BELLA: Yes, I have some, yes.

RONNIE: What exactly?

BELLA: I'm wearing a black silk robe.

[Pause.]

RONNIE: Yes....

BELLA: And some underwear.

[Pause.]

RONNIE: What kind of underwear? *[pause]* Bella?

BELLA: Yes...?

RONNIE: What kind of underwear?

BELLA: French....

RONNIE: French.

BELLA: Yes, French... do you like French, Ronnie? *[pause]* Ronnie?

RONNIE: I love it, Bella. God I love it.

[Bella laughs.]

BELLA: What are you wearing, Ronnie?

RONNIE: Me?

BELLA: Yes.

RONNIE: Oh... *[looking at his filthy vest]* I'm... uh... wearing... a smoking jacket, just my old smoking jacket.

BELLA: That's nice.

RONNIE: Yes... um... Bella?

BELLA: Yes.

RONNIE: Could we meet somewhere? *[pause]* What I mean is... I have so much to say, I... *[pause]* I could love you, Bella.

BELLA: Really, Ron?

RONNIE: Really, Bella.

[Fade in music as Ronnie starts to sing, changing into a morning suit as he does so. Bella, dressed in a wedding dress, stands holding a bleeding heart as Trampas looks on and throws confetti.]

'Hate Street'

I spoke to you on the phone last night after all these years
And you asked me if I was alright and the years just disappeared
And it was as if no time had passed and we were sitting
        once again
In that room, where nothing seemed to last, listening to the rain.
And we were reading different books when you said you realised
That we had, for quite some time been leading separate lives.
The clock was ticking loudly like an unexploded bomb
And I saw then for the first time that your love for me had gone.

I spoke to you on the phone last night and it seemed just like a
        dream.
Your voice was beautiful and light and it entered into me.
And we talked about how young we were, almost children when
        we met.
How we used to cling together in the darkness as we slept.
And we were playing 'Tell the Truth' when you looked at me and
        said
That what we had was yesterday and what we had was dead.

The TV screen was flashing. I looked but could not see.
I sat there in the dying light as it washed all over me.

[Chorus.]
Please don't walk away from me, I want to see your face.
I want to touch your body and I want to share your fate.
The shadows are all falling, I don't want to be alone.
I called around to see you, babe, but you were not at home.

Snow falls on Ynyscedwyn Road, it is written in the stars.
We kiss beneath the mistletoe in the House of Cards.
We kiss beneath the mistletoe by the light of the Christmas trees.
By the dying light of innocence in the nineteen seventies.
Then the miracle was happening and love was all aflame.
And the smoke rose up like angels and the Holy Spirit came.
And we laughed there in the darkness at the stars all peeping
through.
It was twilight down on Hate Street, there was nothing we could
do.

[Chorus.]

> [As the song ends, Ronnie fades into the background
> and Bella looks at a bleeding heart, closely watched by
> Trampas.]

TRAMPAS: I was in love once.

BELLA: Really?

TRAMPAS: Yes. I met her on a busy city street three years last
July. She was carrying groceries piled up to here.
She couldn't see where she was going. I was on the
other side of the street just coming out of the
chemists with a powerful concoction for curing
cold sores when she stepped into the road and
collided with an elderly cyclist who suffered a
heart attack.

BELLA: No.

TRAMPAS: Yes. He never recovered and died on the spot
leaving her with a badly twisted ankle that kept

her off work for a week.

BELLA: Was she compensated?

TRAMPAS: No, but the surviving family suggested that she keep the bike.

BELLA: That's nice.

TRAMPAS: When the commotion was over I took her for a coffee and a fine Danish pastry which was a great stoke of luck because it's through pastries that she connects with her roots.

BELLA: I don't follow you.

TRAMPAS: Her grandfather was from Copenhagen.

BELLA: Ah.

TRAMPAS: Money was no problem to him either. He once paid for us to go on an exotic holiday to the tropics.

BELLA: How lovely. They say the tropics are stunningly beautiful.

TRAMPAS: They are, they are, do you know I once saw a manta a foot under the water twice the size of my duvet.

BELLA: How big is your duvet?

TRAMPAS: That's a leading question.

BELLA: Size isn't everything.

TRAMPAS: No, but it nevertheless is a very big duvet. A passing stranger with the flimsiest knowledge of duvets could tell you that.

BELLA: Are you saying that you'd invite a passing stranger into your bedroom alone to estimate the size of your duvet?

TRAMPAS: Why not?

BELLA: Because of the safety aspect.

TRAMPAS: A drifter is always reckless, Bella.

BELLA: That's as maybe, but in this day and age.

TRAMPAS: I harbour no grudge against the day, but I'm not fond of our age.

BELLA: I agree with you. It is a most difficult one.

TRAMPAS: Especially for love.

BELLA: Love is strange, Trampas.

TRAMPAS: You can say that again.

BELLA: Love is a mystery too.

TRAMPAS: Love is a short-tempered baker and a Danish pastry, Bella.

BELLA: I'm sorry?

TRAMPAS: My love went away with a baker, Royston, a swarthy man with a short temper. I never knew to this day what she saw in him.

BELLA: Some girls like the swarthy, short-tempered baker type, I suppose.

TRAMPAS: He had a windfall, won a lot of money on the pools. He was in a syndicate.

BELLA: They say it's the only way to win the pools.

TRAMPAS: But do you know what I think is odd, weird even, it's that he never, as far as I know, ever wore a moustache.

BELLA: Do you think a moustache would have made any difference?

TRAMPAS: Definitely. She loved a moustache on a man, Bella.

BELLA: Really?

TRAMPAS: Yes. She was in love with Burt Reynolds.

BELLA: No kidding?

TRAMPAS: That's why I grew one.

BELLA: To make her fall in love with you.

TRAMPAS: Exactly and pretend I was the man himself.

BELLA: Did it work?

[Trampas puts on a false moustache.]

TRAMPAS: No. She ran away with Royston without so much as a note.

BELLA: That's tough.

TRAMPAS: It sure is.

BELLA: And now?

TRAMPAS: Now?

BELLA: Is there anyone on the horizon?

TRAMPAS: For me there is no horizon, man, only the indistinct meeting of the sea and sky.

BELLA: That's sad, Trampas, that's really sad.

TRAMPAS: What about you, Bella?

BELLA: I could have flown once but I turned down the offer.

TRAMPAS: That's a shame.

BELLA: I suppose it is.

[Fade in sound of passing aeroplane. Ronnie enters.]

BELLA: It was a Wednesday night. I can remember it like yesterday. I was seventeen. My father locked me in my room; he caught me smoking. My mother brought me haddock with butter and pepper and vinegar. I never touched it. I stared out of the window. I saw Mrs Leandro standing on her doorstep rolling beads between her fingers, came over here after the war from Spain, never spoke a word of the language or if she did, she never spoke it to me. They'd just turned the street lights on, they were turning orange. I watched the drizzle fall to the sound of a blue-bottle banging its head against my window. Then suddenly it stopped. *[pause]* There was silence. Perfect silence. I went to the window, opened it and looked out and knew straightaway that this was the night Martin Bratton would fly. I put on my shoes, climbed out of the window and jumped into the street. The place was deserted. I looked in through the downstairs window and saw my mother knitting and my father asleep in the chair, the weather forecast filling in the background with the hiss of the gas fire. I looked towards his house and started running down the street, across the road through the gate up the path and around to the back where I stopped. The back door was open. I went in. *[pause]* Cabbage boiled on the cooker in the kitchen. In the hall, Mr Bratton was fixing a motorbike. He was covered in oil. He hardly noticed me. I asked him where Martin was but he didn't answer. He just said....

RONNIE: I got into motorbikes on the day Iris lost her marbles, happened like that. One minute she was with us, next, well she took to keeping ferrets. What else could I do?

[Pause.]

BELLA: I smiled and slid past him as he kick-started the machine and pulled away leaving a stream of oil and smoke behind him. *[pause]* I heard the sound of music from upstairs, I couldn't make it out. It sounded like an old song. It reminded me of the days I went to Sunday School in a red velvet dress and red shoes.

[Fade in music at a low level evoking a remembrance of things past.]

BELLA: I climbed to the top of the stairs where I saw a

photo of a man I never knew, a poster of a film I never saw and a Bible lying face down next to a vase of plastic flowers. I knocked at Martin's door but there was no answer, so I turned the handle and walked inside.

[Fade up the music louder as the lights change and Trampas, wrapped in a sheet covered in blood, stands as Martin Bratton.]

BELLA: What's all the blood for?

TRAMPAS: I'm losing my innocence, coming of age. I'm either going to fly or fall from the sky with a crash. *[pause]* You can come with me if you want.

BELLA: I can't.

TRAMPAS: Why not?

BELLA: I'm a virgin and besides, my mother's got some haddock waiting for me on the table.

[Trampas laughs.]

TRAMPAS: You'd better go home then before it gets cold.

BELLA: That's a cruel thing to say, Martin.

TRAMPAS: I can be as cruel as I want. I'm flying away.

BELLA: Nobody flies, Martin.

TRAMPAS: No?

BELLA: No.

TRAMPAS: Then watch this.

[Trampas throws the sheet into the air, to the sound of music. When the sheet hits the floor, the music stops and there is the sound of wind.]

BELLA: I might have loved him. He could have been my friend.

TRAMPAS: It's good to make friends, Bella.

[Fade in music as Ronnie enters and looks east. Trampas lies down and sleeps.]

RONNIE: I still love you, Bella.

BELLA: Really, Ron?

RONNIE: Really, Bella.

BELLA: Since when?

RONNIE: The day I saw you walk naked into the river apart from your shoes.

BELLA: It was a hot day.

RONNIE: It was a lovely day.

BELLA: It was a summer's day.

RONNIE: I loved you then, Bella.

BELLA: The river stones hurt my feet.

RONNIE: Your breasts were heavy and white.

BELLA: I needed a holiday.

RONNIE: Your nipples were hard.

BELLA: The river was cold.

RONNIE: You let your hair down over your shoulders.

BELLA: I'd forgotten to wash it, it needed a wash.

RONNIE: I watched you swim.

BELLA: You should have come in.

RONNIE: I couldn't swim.

BELLA: But you can now.

RONNIE: I couldn't then and we are talking about then....

BELLA: I could have fucked you then.

RONNIE: And now?

BELLA: With my shoes on.

RONNIE: Bella?

BELLA: In the river.

RONNIE: Bella....

BELLA: With my hardened nipples and heavy breasts.

RONNIE: BELLA! You are not listening to me!

BELLA: You were afraid.

RONNIE: I wasn't.

BELLA: Of me.

RONNIE: Of water.

BELLA: You should have come in.

RONNIE: I paddled, you saw me paddle.

BELLA: I did but I was already out on the other side.

RONNIE: You could have come back.

BELLA: I was breathless.

RONNIE: We were supposed to be together.

BELLA: The water parted us.

RONNIE: It was only a river.

BELLA: Perhaps a symbol.

RONNIE: The river? Of what?

BELLA: Who knows?

RONNIE: Don't talk shit.

BELLA: I am not talking shit.

RONNIE: Everything's a symbol according to you.

BELLA: Perhaps everything is.

RONNIE: But what if everything isn't?

BELLA: Then I would have made a mistake.

RONNIE: So then what would you say?

BELLA: I'd say I'd ruined my shoes for a swim in a meaningless river for which you call me a fool and we sit on the bank a few minutes later eating a picnic in silence and drinking.

RONNIE: Champagne.

BELLA: What?

RONNIE: I bought champagne that day, I remember going up to the counter with the bottle asking for fags when....

BELLA: What?

RONNIE: There was a snag.

BELLA: A hitch?

RONNIE: A balls up.

BELLA: How typical.

RONNIE: I only left my wallet in the suitcase, Bella.

BELLA: So there was no champagne.

[Lights fade on Bella and Trampas, leaving Ronnie alone.]

RONNIE: Not quite. I found a tenner in my top left hand pocket. I must have left it there the day I got pissed on International day, we lost 12-10. Alastair McHarg broke his ribs, a bloke standing next to me fell over and broke his ankle bad, it was a compound fracture, the same kind of fracture Ian Hall had during our midweek defeat by the All Blacks in 1974 when Ian Kirkpatrick picked the ball up at the base of the scrum, ran straight for a try past Phil Bennet under the posts. *[pause]* The crowd went quiet, Bella, I've never heard such a silent crowd. It was AS IF THERE WAS NO ONE THERE.

*[Ronnie looks around realizing that Bella has gone.
Fade in the sound of an express train passing which
drowns out Ronnie's cries.]*

RONNIE: BELLA, BELLA, BELLA!

*[Ronnie exits. Trampas stands and watches as the train
noise fades away.]*

TRAMPAS: The iron horse from the city moves away relentlessly over the snowy plains of a silent country.

BELLA: That's nice, Trampas.

TRAMPAS: Do you like it?

BELLA: Yes, you should have been a poet.

TRAMPAS: Wymff always said I was.

BELLA: Wymff?

TRAMPAS: He was a friend of mine. We grew up together. We were like brothers. No one could ever separate Wymff and me. We were like that. *[crossing his fingers] [pause]* He was a miner. Miners are hard as nails.

BELLA: It's a shame it died out... mining.

TRAMPAS: It is.

BELLA: It's a real shame.

TRAMPAS: Miners used to bring down governments.

BELLA: They did.

TRAMPAS: There were thousands of them.

BELLA: Yes.

TRAMPAS: Pits all over the place.

BELLA: And now there's none.

TRAMPAS: None.

BELLA: None.

TRAMPAS: Just holes in the ground.

BELLA: It's funny.

TRAMPAS: It is.

BELLA: Hard to believe.

TRAMPAS: Yes.

BELLA: But true.

TRAMPAS: Yes. All true. *[pause]* Wymff had no choice but to go to the city. I went with him.

BELLA: The city?

TRAMPAS: Yeah, the city.

> *[Lights change. Fade in music as Ronnie starts to sing. The next sequence should suggest Trampas' transformation from hometown boy to a lost soul in a fallen city, a humbling and humiliating experience. He may sing the last verse until it disintegrates to nothing — a truly painful experience.]*

'Talking About You And Me'

I'm not talking about the Glittering City
I'm not talking about the Sparkling Bridge
I'm not talking about disfigurement
I'm not talking about the violins
I'm not talking about the smell of rum and coca cola
I'm not talking about the girl in the pretty dress
I'm not talking about the twilight
Though it was a thing of loveliness.

[Chorus.]
I'm just talking about you and me.

I'm not talking about the Sparkling Darkness
I'm not talking about the Strawberry Fields
I'm not talking about a Clockwork Orange
I'm not talking about a Tangerine Dream
I'm not talking about Jack the Ripper
I'm not talking about a monkey on a stick

I'm not talking about the Big Dipper
Though it frightened me and made me sick.

[Chorus.]

I'm not talking about the swimming pool
I'm not talking about the emotional crush
I'm not talking about the bandages
I'm not talking about the Shrine of Love
I'm not talking about the Wedding Dress
I'm not talking about the moon and the stars
I'm not talking about the Resurrection
Or the diamonds or the lilac stars.

[Chorus.]

I'm not talking about the cult of beauty
I'm not talking about the tower blocks
I'm not talking about evolution
I'm not talking about the multi-storey car park
I'm not talking about the cabaret show
I'm not talking about narcotic love on dark settees
I'm not talking about fairy lights in café windows
Ah but it looks so lovely.

[Chorus.]

[The song ends. Trampas is alone. Ronnie walks into the shadows. Silence.]

TRAMPAS: *[pause]* I thought I could be somebody, that's all, that I'd make it... get re-born, start again. *[pause]* I thought the stars would shine down on me and it would be there, in front of me, within grasp, reachable, to be had, felt, taken in hand and held, squeezed, there in front of me, a light flickering, a good thing, not far away, mine... *[pause]* I wanted it bad... *[pause]* I once thought I saw it. *[pause]* I put out my arms, I opened them, I shut my eyes expecting a touch, on my lips, in my mind, I once thought it touched the tips of my fingers and I think I smiled, you know the way you smile when something good is going to happen? Is on the verge of happening so close you can really smell it? A perfume, a strange perfume, a wisp, a tail, a stream of smoke coiling around me, a serpent hissing, strange perfume in the boots of cars, buses, faces, my eyes are shut, my lips right over my teeth and music, strange music, like I imagine tomorrow's song, song of tomorrow, my head is on fire, I feel as if I'm burning, my skin is melting, my fingers reach, are reaching, I could have been, I nearly did, I saw it as clear as day. *[pause]*

Then I opened my eyes on the bitter silence of now. *[pause]* Maybe I opened my eyes too soon. Maybe I should have waited, I had time, I mean, I'm not that old, I was so near, I was so fucking near then it was gone... do you know what I'm saying? *[pause]* I told Wymff I was going home. At first he said nothing, then he laughed and said, "Home?". I said "Yes, home, what's wrong with that?" *[pause]* He stubbed out his fag in the ashtray and said "You haven't got a home man," he said, "it don't exist, it disappeared, it shrunk, it fucked off, it took a walk, it died, it no longer continued to be." *[pause]* I finished my drink, walked out of the pub and I haven't seen him since. And I don't think I ever will again.

[Pause. Trampas turns to Bella.]

TRAMPAS: I could love you, Bella. I could get rid of Ronnie and we could live together.

BELLA: No, Trampas.

TRAMPAS: I'll build a new house.

BELLA: Trampas, listen to me.

TRAMPAS: A house of love, here, me, you, East from the Gantry.

BELLA: You're not listening to me.

TRAMPAS: I can kill for love, Bella, I....

BELLA: Shut up, Trampas, please.

TRAMPAS: Why can't you love me?

            [Pause.]

BELLA: I don't know.

TRAMPAS: I'm a very lonely person, Bella.

BELLA: I know... I'd better go.

TRAMPAS: Is it because I don't know who I am... Bella?

            [Pause.]

BELLA: You'll find someone somewhere, but not me, not
            this time, it can't be me.

            *[Bella exits, Trampas lights a lighter and we see and
            hear a roaring fire. Bella and Ronnie enter into cold blue
            light. Bella stands looking east. Ronnie watches her. Sil-
            ence.]*

BELLA: They say it's general.

RONNIE: What is?

BELLA: The snow.

RONNIE: Jesus Christ.

BELLA: Don't you think it's effective for making the ugliest
            thing attractive, even beautiful!

RONNIE: No.

BELLA: A few days ago, I walked past the old iron works
            on Ynyscedwyn Road. I was struck by its fierce, if
            bleak, beauty, the dereliction was overwhelming,
            the falling snow a balm of forgetfulness, I called
            into the tavern for a drink. I lit a cigarette and
            stood by the window.

RONNIE: Fucking hell.

BELLA: I looked up at the TV set in the corner, the weather-
            man said there would be drifts. I think his name

was Michael Fish.

RONNIE: Who is Michael Fish?

BELLA: The weatherman.

RONNIE: What did he look like?

BELLA: He had a moustache and glasses and a sort of greeny brown check sports jacket.

RONNIE: Is that all?

BELLA: I think so yes, why?

RONNIE: I don't believe you, that's why.

BELLA: I saw him clearly, Ronnie.

RONNIE: No weatherman worth his salt would forecast a snow drift wearing only a sports jacket, glasses and a moustache. What the fuck do you take me for, Bella?

BELLA: I didn't mean that's all he had on, Ronnie.

RONNIE: But that's what you said.

BELLA: I was just outlining his most distinctive characteristics that's all, I....

RONNIE: Since when has a greeny brown check sports jacket ever been distinctive?

BELLA: Never.

RONNIE: Exactly.

BELLA: But it's not what I meant.

RONNIE: I think you fantasize about him.

BELLA: What?

RONNIE: Has he got a big penis, is that it?

BELLA: Ronnie.

RONNIE: Is he circumcised?

BELLA: I'm not going to...

RONNIE: Will you take him as a lover?... quickly, passionately, on the floor?... with the weather signs above your head?... will you, Bella, will you?

BELLA: You're insane, Ronnie.

RONNIE: I know, but you're the one who turns a perfectly innocuous television weather forecast into lurid fantasy, not me.

BELLA: There was no lurid fantasy, I....

RONNIE: There was. YOU IMAGINED MICHAEL FISH NAKED, you imagined that he was talking just to you, enticing you with soft words of snowdrifts, he probably knew how much you love the snow, how effective you think snow is for making the ugliest thing attractive, even beautiful, he took advantage of you, Bella, caught you at your weakest, when I wasn't around, he's a bastard, Bella, a complete and utter bastard and you're no better because you probably egged him on.

BELLA: I did not egg him on, Ron, I was having a quiet drink in a cosy tavern with a few afternoon customers studying 'The Sporting Life' in front of a roaring fire.

RONNIE: How can you talk about a roaring fire in front of me?

BELLA: What?

RONNIE: When you burnt down our house!

BELLA: That is outrageous. IT WAS AN ACCIDENT.

RONNIE: If only you'd come to bed when I called you.

BELLA: I was watching a film.

RONNIE: Smoking a cigarette.

BELLA: That is no crime, Ronnie.

RONNIE: It is when you burn down a house and almost everything in it.

BELLA: The cigarette was not the cause.

RONNIE: That's not what the fireman said.

BELLA: The fireman could only speculate.

RONNIE: HE IS A PROFESSIONAL MAN.

BELLA: IT COULD HAVE BEEN ELECTRICAL.

RONNIE: And how come it was I who discovered the fire?

BELLA: I went for a walk. I needed some air.

RONNIE: But you said it was a horror film.

BELLA: It was.

RONNIE: You said it scared you out of your wits.

BELLA: It did.

RONNIE: Then why did you go for a walk when you were scared out of your wits and petrified?

BELLA: I have never been afraid of walking the mountains at dark!

RONNIE: BOLLOCKS, BELLA, BOLLOCKS!

BELLA: How many more times must we go over this, Ronnie?

RONNIE: Until I find out the truth.

BELLA: The truth is....

RONNIE: That you started the fire deliberately.

BELLA: That you are a jealous bastard.

RONNIE: I am not, I....

BELLA: Then why the fuck else did you shoot that cat?

RONNIE: It was an accident.

BELLA: You are a jealous and paranoid bastard, Ronnie,

and you know it.

RONNIE: It was a mistake, Bella.

BELLA: It was no mistake, Ronnie, you never gave it a chance.

RONNIE: I....

BELLA: Boom, boom, Ronnie John, comes out of his lair like a frightened rabbit in his underpants with his gun in his hands and blows the poor thing to smithereens. THERE WAS NOTHING LEFT OF IT, RONNIE.

RONNIE: I over-reacted, Bella, that's all.

BELLA: That's all.

RONNIE: Besides, I never shot him in my pants. I had my trousers on.

BELLA: Oh good God, that makes all the difference, does it?

RONNIE: No, but you never let me explain, I....

BELLA: There is nothing to explain, Ronnie, it was cold-blooded MURDER you....

RONNIE: I THOUGHT IT WAS MARTIN BRATTON.

[Silence.]

BELLA: What?

RONNIE: You heard.

BELLA: I don't believe it.

RONNIE: It's the truth.

BELLA: Are you mad?

RONNIE: I am but on this occasion it's got nothing to do with what happened.

BELLA: But you said....

RONNIE: It was my dream that gave him away.

BELLA: What dream?

RONNIE: It was a clear day....

[Fade in music low level, lights change.]

The house was rebuilt with ranch fencing all around it, two apple trees in flower stand on one side, a hammock is suspended in the middle and I am dozing in it. I am wearing shorts, my legs are sunburned, a book rests on my chest, a cool drink sits on a small table nearby. I listen to the sound of a bee buzzing from the depths of a purple foxglove which we planted together the year before. I watch you approach in a white dress, you are playing with the stalk of a flower, you are smiling. You are carrying a musical box which you lay on the table next to the hammock. You open the box and some music plays and a dancer goes round and round in a mirror. Perhaps she is admiring herself. *[sound of the musical box]* You put your hand on the inside of my thigh, your fingers are cool, you are stroking me gently, you undo the buttons on my shorts and move your hand inside, slowly, slowly. You are driving me wild with desire, I reach up to your breast. I stoke it, my lips are dry, your nipples erect, you take my heavy cock in your hands, I am on fire, I am.... *[the music stops]* The music stops, my hand stops, the bee leaves the foxglove, the ice melts in my drink and the novel falls from my chest to the floor with a thud. Foolishly I ask you whether you would like to make love or pay a visit to the garden centre to get a new fan belt for the lawn mower. And you laugh, like you are laughing now and then summer turns to winter and the snow begins to fall. *[snow falls]* You take your hand away and walk back towards the house. I follow you to bed but before I turn out the light, I look out at the snow-covered landscape. And then I saw him. Out in the field in the back, he was leaning against a tree, smoking, watching the house. I ran downstairs to get my gun but by the time I got there he was gone. *[pause]* I thought he'd come back for you, Bella, but he isn't going to get you.

BELLA: It wasn't Martin Bratton, Ronnie.

RONNIE: It was, he was your first love and you are still in love with him.

BELLA: No, Ronnie.

RONNIE: You said he'd come back for you, you said you saw him fly east from the gantry.

BELLA: I know what I said, Ronnie, but he never made it.

RONNIE: What?

BELLA: He's dead, Ronnie.

[Fade in music at low level.]

I went home to my house, to eat my haddock. I told my parents what I saw. "Martin Bratton's flown away," I said. "No he hasn't," said my father, "he jumped out of his bedroom window and killed himself. It's been on the news, isn't that right, Beth?" "Your father's right," said my mother, "We heard the ambulance driver speaking to a reporter. The man reading the news said teenage suicides were rising. I put it down to all this snow." "It's not true, Mam," I said, "I saw him fly east from the gantry." *[pause]* My mother and father looked at each other before calling the doctor to me and giving me a sweet cup of tea. "She's in shock," they told the doctor, "She saw it happen. He was her boyfriend". The doctor said he thought it was sad and then my mother said that they thought it was sad too.

[Pause. Music fades.]

RONNIE: I'm sorry, Bella.

BELLA: Forget it.

RONNIE;   I didn't mean to....

BELLA: No.

[Bella moves away from him.]

RONNIE: Then who was it I saw in the snow?

BELLA: That was probably Trampas.

RONNIE: Trampas?

BELLA: Trampas.

[Fade in music as Trampas enters. Music fades. All three look at each other for a moment. It is an uneasy silence.]

BELLA: Ronnie, Trampas. Trampas, Ronnie.

RONNIE: Hello, Trampas.

TRAMPAS: Hello, Ronnie.

BELLA: I was thinking, perhaps Trampas would like to stay for dinner with us Ron.

RONNIE: Dinner... yes... yes.

TRAMPAS: Are you sure?

BELLA: Positive, aren't we, Ron?

RONNIE: Yes... yes.

BELLA: Besides we ordered a king-size pizza not long ago. There'll be plenty for three.

TRAMPAS: Well, I don't want to impose.

BELLA: You're not imposing at all, is he, Ron?

RONNIE: No... no... do you like pepperoni, Trampas?

TRAMPAS: Umm... yes.

BELLA: We ordered pepperoni instead of anchovy. I hope you don't mind.

TRAMPAS: No, no... it's one of my favourite toppings.

BELLA: So that's settled then.

TRAMPAS: Yes... thank you.

BELLA: Ronnie has a theory about pizza eaters see, Trampas.

RONNIE: Yes... I....

BELLA: He thinks that he can tell the sort of person somebody is by the pizza they buy.

TRAMPAS: Is that right, Ronnie?

BELLA: Yes, he made a study of it, haven't you, Ronnie?

RONNIE: Yes, I suppose I have, I....

BELLA: Often people who want loads of toppings on a deep pan pizza are filling a void in their lives and those who want a plain cheese and tomato thin crust are more contented.

TRAMPAS: That's an interesting theory.

RONNIE: Those who order artichoke like the exotic. Do you like the exotic, Trampas?

BELLA: Would anyone like a drink?

RONNIE: That would be a nice idea.

BELLA: Beer, Trampas?

TRAMPAS: Yeah.

BELLA: The beer's in the fridge, Ronnie.

[Bella goes to lay the table. The two men stand in silence.]

RONNIE: So you were in 'The Virginian' then?

TRAMPAS: No.

RONNIE: That's a pity. I've never met a TV star before.

TRAMPAS: I'm not really a TV star, Ronnie.

RONNIE: Just a saddle tramp looking for a home, huh?

TRAMPAS: Something like that.

RONNIE: If you ask me you look more like Burt Reynolds
            than Trampas. Trampas, put a moustache on you,
            you'd be a dead ringer.

TRAMPAS: Really.

RONNIE: Yes. Do you like Burt Reynolds, Trampas?

TRAMPAS: Not particularly.

RONNIE: I do. I think he's a god. What is your favourite
            film?

TRAMPAS: 'Citizen Kane'.

RONNIE: Burt Reynolds isn't in 'Citizen Kane', Orson Welles
            is.

TRAMPAS: I know.

RONNIE: So what are you saying?

TRAMPAS: I'm saying that 'Citizen Kane' is my favourite film,
            that's all.

RONNIE: But Burt Reynolds isn't in it, mun.

TRAMPAS: I know Burt Reynolds isn't in it, mun.

RONNIE: But I wanted you to tell me which of Burt Rey-
            nolds' films you like the best.

TRAMPAS: None, alright. I think all Burt Reynolds' films are
            crap.

RONNIE: What about 'Deliverance'.

TRAMPAS: What about it.

RONNIE: It's a good film.

TRAMPAS: I think it's crap.

RONNIE: Really? What about the Southern inbred kid with
            the banjo?

TRAMPAS: How do you know he's inbred?

BELLA: *[moving downstage]* I don't think Trampas is interested in talking about films, Ronnie.

RONNIE: I was....

BELLA: Are you, Trampas?

TRAMPAS: Not really, no.

RONNIE: Oh, and there was me thinking he was a buff.

[Pause.]

BELLA: Trampas has come a long way. I don't think he's up to a discussion.

RONNIE: I'm sorry, Trampas.

TRAMPAS: Forget it, Ronnie.

BELLA: Ronnie can get very carried away sometimes you see, Trampas, can't you, Ron?

[Pause.]

RONNIE: Yes, yes I suppose I can, but then it's a crazy world full of crazy people.

BELLA: Absolutely.

[Bella continues to lay the table.]

TRAMPAS: She's a remarkable woman, Ronnie.

RONNIE: Yes, but she can be prone to the strangest behaviour.

TRAMPAS: Really?

RONNIE: Yes, I think she burnt down our home.

[Pause.]

TRAMPAS: How strange.

RONNIE: It is, isn't it, but then again, I suppose we'll rebuild it one day, make it good and strong and open, so that when we have visitors, we can entertain them properly.

TRAMPAS: It might be a long job, Ron.

RONNIE: I know, but who knows, with a bit of help, I could do it, start again, here, east from the Gantry. It might be a good place one day, Trampas. That's my dream.

TRAMPAS: That's good, Ron.

[Pause.]

RONNIE: Have you got a home, Trampas?

TRAMPAS: Not any more. The home I knew has gone forever.

RONNIE: Time to make a new start then.

TRAMPAS: Something like that. The first thing I'll do is change my name.

RONNIE: What's your real name?

TRAMPAS: My real name is Billy.

RONNIE: Call yourself Billy then.

TRAMPAS: I guess I will.

RONNIE: Hello, Billy.

TRAMPAS: Hello, Ronnie.

[They shake hands.]

RONNIE: You couldn't have loved Bella, see Billy.

TRAMPAS: No?

RONNIE: No.

TRAMPAS: Why not?

RONNIE: She's in love with Michael Fish.

TRAMPAS: Who's Michael Fish?

RONNIE: Just a weatherman.

TRAMPAS: Oh.

[Fade in music. Ronnie leads Trampas to the table. Bella pours some wine and lights some candles. The table looks beautifully laid, ready for something good to happen. They toast. Music and light fades.]

FINISH

The Author

Edward Thomas was born in Abercrâf, Swansea Valley and is a founder member and artistic director of Y Cwmni Cyf Theatre in Cardiff. He has acted, written and directed extensively for radio, film, television and the theatre. His most recent work for television includes *A Silent Village/Pentre Mud*, a fifty minute documentary for the BBC/S4C, and *Fallen Sons*, a thirty minute film for Wales Playhouse, both of which won Celtic Film Festival Awards in 1994. In addition to this New Wales Trilogy of plays he has written *Adar Heb Adenydd* (1989), *The Myth Of Michael Roderick* (1990), *Envy* (1991) and *Strangers In Conversation* (1993). In 1993 he won an Arts Foundation Fellowship and the BBC Writer of the Year Award. His new play, *A Song From A Forgotten City* won a Barclays New Stages Award in 1994 and will open in Cardiff in February, 1995.

House Of America won a Time Out/01 For London Award in 1989. *Flowers Of The Dead Red Sea* has been adapted for BBC Radio 3 Drama and was broadcast in June, 1992 and was also adapted as a libretto for composer John Hardy whose piece was produced by Music Theatre Wales in March, 1993.

Note To The Series

Welsh drama found a new and distinctive voice in the eighties. Before that, there were new theatres in Wales, but there was little new drama. Why was it that there was a surge of new writing at this time? Perhaps it is no accident that the decade was one of economic hardship and unemployment. It would not be the first time that adversity has brought the best out of the Welsh. We can be certain, however, that new writers were sustained by the commitment of a band of theatre professionals, many of whom shared with them a common background and experience. During this period, new writers have been specifically fostered by the Made in Wales Stage Company. This academy of stage writing has had a crucial training role, enabling emerging dramatists to learn through workshops and the experience of seeing their plays performed in front of an audience. Other companies, such as Hijinx, The Sherman Theatre, Theatre Clwyd, Moving Being, Y Cwmni, and others, have commissioned new plays and/or taken them to community venues to people who would normally find theatres alien and intimidating. Welsh dramatists have benefited directly from this professional support system and indirectly from the patronage of public bodies but they have not yet reached the audiences that they deserve. Irish theatre-goers have in the past greeted new writers with riots, and today they still provide the oxygen of controversy, but if the attendance at some Welsh premieres is any indication, innovation in Wales meets with indifference from the public at large.

Seren, with the support of the Arts Council of Wales, are pleased to publish a series of new plays which will facilitate re-staging, enhance the status of new dramatists, and, we hope,

215

help draw new audiences into our theatres. We cannot afford, nor would it be proper, to limit support to a movement or faction, if any exists. To the list of writers who were born in Wales, or who now live here, we will add the name of any writer of quality, who makes his or her initial breakthrough before Welsh audiences.

There are a number of questions that need to be answered about the present state of our theatre. Just how good are our writers? Is the neglect of English managements evidence of discrimination, or merely of lack of knowledge? Are we at last beginning to create a national theatre that will one day equal those of Scotland and Ireland? We hope that the publication of this drama series will help to find the answers.

Brian Mitchell
Editor